# Two-Hour Party Cakes

*30 cakes to decorate
in two hours or less*

# Two-Hour Party Cakes

## CAROL DEACON

*Cakes to decorate in two hours or less*

# Contents

# Introduction

The trouble with birthdays, anniversaries and Christmas is that they keep on coming. Just when you think you've made the ultimate cake for a celebration, another occasion appears on the horizon and you're back to square one, thinking "What on earth shall I make for them this year?"

Hopefully, this book will inspire you with enough suggestions and ideas to keep all your family and friends in cakes for a long time to come, with the minimum of fuss or purchase of expensive cake-decorating equipment on your part. You should have little problem in decorating the cakes in this book in two hours, but if you want to bake your own cake, you will need to allow more time. There are also some decorating techniques which will benefit from a little extra time (when using gelatin icing as on the Fairy-tale Castle, for example) but these are exceptions.

Feel free to alter and adapt the designs or invent shortcuts wherever you wish. For instance, if you are in a hurry and don't wish to cover a cake board, then simply leave it plain. If you don't have time to make a lot of characters, then just make one. If you have another technique you are more familiar with, perhaps for making roses, use that instead of the one I suggest. There is no ultimate "right" way of doing things – just use the method you feel happiest with and make your own unique creation.

Above all, don't be scared to say something new. At the end of the day, it's just cake and frosting, and if it really starts to cause problems, just eat it!

*Carol Deacon*

# Fairy-tale castle

*Although this cake is a lot easier to make than it looks, you do have to allow drying time for the turrets (preferably overnight). Once you have mastered gelatin icing, a whole new world of standing models opens up.*

1 Begin by making the turrets. Cover all the cardboard tubes with plastic wrap and dust lightly with cornstarch. Make up the gelatin icing as shown on page 99 and place in a plastic bag. Dust the work surface with cornstarch. Pull off a lump of icing about 4¼ oz and roll out no thicker than ⅛ in. Cut out a rectangle about 5½ in x 6½ in . Place the excess icing back in the bag.

Wrap the icing around one of the thicker tubes and secure the join with a little water *(fig 1)*. Place to dry (seam side down) on a spare cake board or similar.

Make another four the same size and one shorter one using the thinner tube. The smaller turret should be about 3 in in length.

After about 4-6 hours of drying, the turrets should feel hard on the outside. Carefully slide them off their supports and stand them upright so the centers can dry out. Leave overnight.

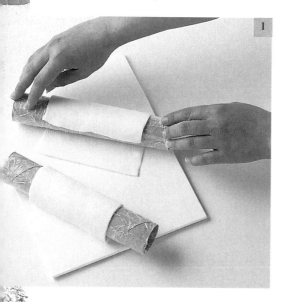

2 Level the top of the cake and place it upside down in the middle of the board. Slice and fill the center with butter cream. Spread a thin layer of butter cream over the top and sides.

3 Dust the work surface with confectioner's sugar. Roll out and cover the cake with 1 lb 2 oz of white ready-to-roll fondant. Smooth the top and sides and trim any excess from the base. Press a clean ruler horizontally three or four times around the sides of the cake *(fig 2)*. Then use the back of a knife to make vertical marks for the bricks.

4 When dry, place a long and short turret together on top of the cake. Insure the seams are at the back and secure them using classic fondant icing. To provide extra support, roll 1 oz of white ready-to-roll fondant into a sausage about 11 in long. Paint a light line of water around the base of the two turrets and, starting from the back, press the sausage in place *(fig 3)*.

5 To make two doors, thinly roll out the brown ready-to-roll fondant and cut out two rounded, arched shapes. Press a few vertical lines into each one with the back of a knife. Stick the largest door on the front of the cake and the other on the front of the tallest turret. Make two steps in front of each door by sticking two small ovals of

## INGREDIENTS

- 1 quantity gelatin icing (see page 99)
- Cornstarch
- 7-inch round sponge cake (see pages 94-97)
- 1 quantity butter cream (see page 98)
- Confectioner's sugar
- 1 lb 8 oz white ready-to-roll fondant
- ¼ oz brown ready-to-roll fondant
- 1¾ oz black ready-to-roll fondant
- 1 quantity white classic fondant icing (see page 99)
- 2 edible silver balls
- 25 mini-marshmallows
- 6 ice cream cones
- Two 1-oz bags white chocolate buttons or similar
- Green food coloring (ideally gooseberry green but not essential)
- 1 sheet rice paper
- 2½ oz green-colored coconut (see page 98)

## UTENSILS

- 6 cardboard tubes (5 kitchen roll inner tubes and one from a roll of aluminum foil are ideal. Please don't use toilet rolls!)
- Plastic wrap
- Rolling pin
- Small sharp knife
- Water and paintbrush
- Carving knife
- 12-in square cake board
- Ruler
- 4 piping bags (minimum)
- Number 2 piping nozzle
- Scissors
- Small strainer

**4**

white fondant on top of each other *(fig 4)*. Stick an edible silver ball on the front of each door with a little classic fondant icing.

6 Stick about 25 mini-marshmallows around the perimeter of the cake with classic fondant icing. (If you cannot find mini-marshmallows in the supermarket, cut up a sausage of fondant instead.)

7 Take two of the ice cream cones. Break little pieces off the base if necessary to help them stand upright. Pipe a thin line of classic fondant icing around the top edges of both turrets and then stick the cones carefully in place on top.

　You may find that you have to break a little "bite" shape out of one side of the cone that goes on top of the shorter turret

so that it can sit snugly against the taller turret *(fig 5)*.

8 Neaten the base of each cone with a line of white chocolate buttons stuck on with dabs of classic fondant icing.

9 Place the four remaining gelatin cylinders around the cake. Secure with classic fondant icing and top each one with a cone and line of buttons as before.

10 To make the windows on the turrets, thinly roll out the black ready-to-roll fondant and cut out eight narrow rectangles. Keep the leftover fondant. Cut one end of each rectangle into a point. Stick one on each turret and two either side of the front door.
　Place a little white classic fondant icing in a piping bag fitted with the number 2 nozzle. Pipe a neat line from the top to the bottom of a window *(fig 6)*. Then pipe a line across the window. Repeat on all the rest. (Leave the windows bare if you find this too tricky.)

**6**

**5**

**TIP**

*If the cake is for someone's birthday, make some extra rocks. Stick them at the front of the board to use as candle holders.*

11 To make the rocks, partially knead together 4 oz white ready-to-roll fondant and ¼ oz of black. Pull off irregular lumps and stick these on the board around the cake using a little water.

12 Color 3 tbsp classic fondant icing green. Place half into a piping bag fitted with the number 2 piping nozzle and pipe wiggly lines for the ivy stems all over the cake. Place the rest of the icing in a second bag and snip ⅛ in off the end of the bag. Press the end of the bag against a stem, squeeze lightly, then pull the bag away. This should make a simple leaf shape. Continue all over the cake. Practice this first on a sheet of waxed paper if you are not very confident.

13 To make the flags, cut six small triangles out of the sheet of rice paper. Pipe a dot of classic fondant icing on the top of one of the cones. Stick a small ball of ready-to-roll fondant on top and pipe another dot on top of that. Press one of the triangles into the fondant (*fig 7*). Repeat on the other five cones.

14 Moisten the exposed cake board with water and sprinkle the colored coconut around the base of the cake. To add snow, place a spoonful of confectioner's sugar in a small strainer and sprinkle over the cake.

# Decorating variation

In this simplified version there are only four turrets instead of six, which saves you time. Also, instead of piping leaves, I have used cut-out flowers and leaves which look just as good. You could also place little figures in front of the top turrets. Use the couple featured on the Bride and Groom cake on page 57 for instance and it turns into a stunning wedding cake with a difference.

# Hot dog

*How do you like yours? With or without mustard ...
er... sorry, frosting! Here's one mega bite-sized dog complete
with all the trimmings that should satisfy a whole army of hungry
party goers.*

### ■ INGREDIENTS

- Confectioner's sugar for rolling out
- 6¼ oz dark blue ready-to-roll fondant
- Oblong sponge cake baked in loaf pan (see page 94)
- I quantity butter cream (see page 98)
- I lb 12 oz light golden brown ready-to-roll fondant
- Assorted food color pastes for painting hot dog (see step 5)
- 3½ oz white ready-to-roll fondant
- I tbsp yellow-colored butter cream or classic fondant icing
- I tbsp red-colored butter cream or classic fondant icing (see pages 98-99)

### ■ UTENSILS

- Water and paintbrush
- Rolling pin
- Small sharp knife
- Carving knife
- Palette or saucer
- 2 piping bags (see page 102)
- Scissors

1 Cover the cake board with blue ready-to-roll fondant as described on page 100. Trim and neaten the edges. Place the covered board to one side. Stand the cake the right way up and cut a groove lengthwise out of the center *(fig 1)*.

2 Round the corners slightly and cut away any rough, uneven bits of cake from the tops and sides. Slice and spread a layer of butter cream in the center of the cake if you wish. Carefully reassemble the cake and spread butter cream over the top and sides and into the groove.

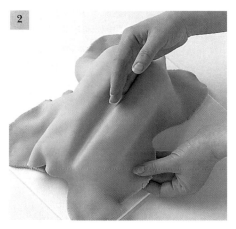

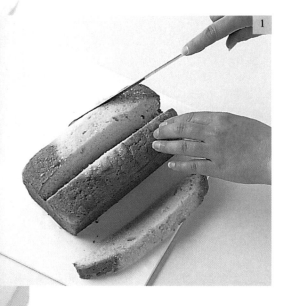

3 Still keeping the cake away from the covered board, knead 1 lb 5 oz of the brown ready-to-roll fondant until pliable. Roll it out on a surface well dusted with confectioner's sugar, then lift and place over the cake, allowing the fondant to fall into the dip in the middle as much as possible. Starting from the middle of the cake to expel as much air as possible, smooth and ease the fondant into position *(fig 2)*. Neaten the sides and trim away any excess from the base. Keep the leftover fondant to add to the hot dog later.

4 Carefully lift and place the cake on the covered board. Choose the side that looks best and press about six diagonal lines into that side using the back of a knife.

5 Roll the leftover brown fondant into a thick wiener shape, then lay this across the dip. Press a few lines into the ends of the wiener with the back of a knife, and to give it a luscious just-cooked look paint the wiener using food colorings. I found a mixture of watered-down dark brown, chestnut and autumn leaf food coloring pastes worked well, but you could achieve the same effect by mixing brown with a touch of yellow, red or orange.

6 For the napkin, thinly roll out the white ready-to-roll fondant and cut two strips 11 in x 3 in. Moisten the board and the base of the cake. Take one strip and lay it down one side of hot dog, allowing it to fall into folds. Repeat on the other side.

7 Make up two piping bags. Place the yellow-colored classic fondant icing or butter cream in one bag and the red in the other. Pipe a long squiggly line of yellow "mustard" along the top of the wiener *(fig 3)*. Repeat using the red "catsup."

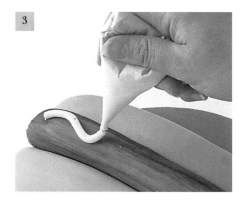

### TIP
*You may be able to find packs containing small tubes of red and yellow "writing icing" in your local supermarket, which could be used for the mustard and catsup. Snip a little extra off the end of the tube to make the nozzle wider.*

# Handyman

*Although this was designed with do-it-yourself fanatics in mind, this would make a good cake for someone who's just moved house and has all the joys of decorating ahead! Personalize the figure to resemble the recipient if you can.*

### INGREDIENTS

- 6-in square sponge cake (see pages 94–97)
- 1 quantity butter cream (see page 98)
- Confectioner's sugar for rolling out
- 1 lb 2 oz white ready-to-roll fondant
- 3 oz blue ready-to-roll fondant
- ¾ oz flesh-colored ready-to-roll fondant
- Black food coloring paste
- 1 oz black ready-to-roll fondant
- ¼ oz gray ready-to-roll fondant
- 3¾ oz dark brown ready-to-roll fondant

### UTENSILS

- Carving knife
- 8-inch-square cake board
- Cake spatula
- Small sharp knife
- Water and fine and medium paintbrushes
- Piping nozzle

1 Level the top of the cake, turn it upside down and place in the center of the board. Slice the cake in half and fill the center with butter cream. Reassemble the cake and spread a thin covering of butter cream around the top and sides.

2 Knead and roll out 14 oz white ready-to-roll fondant on a work surface dusted with confectioner's sugar. Carefully lay the fondant over the cake. Smooth the fondant into place and trim and neaten the base.

3 To construct the handyman himself, begin with the body. Roll 1¼ oz of white ready-to-roll fondant into a cone *(fig 1)*. Paint a little water in the middle of the cake and place his body in position. Next make his legs by rolling 1¼ oz of blue ready-to-roll fondant into a sausage 7 in long. Cut the sausage in half and bend the left leg slightly at the knee. Stick the legs in front of the body. For the arms, roll ¾ oz of white fondant into a thin sausage and cut it in half. Stick these either side of the handyman's body.

4 To make his head, use ¼ oz flesh-colored ready-to-roll fondant and roll this into a ball. Slice a little fondant off the top of his head to make a flat surface on which to attach the cap. Stick the head on top of the body. Flatten two tiny balls of white fondant and stick these onto his face for his eyes. Add a tiny ball of flesh-colored fondant for his nose. Paint the pupils on the eyes and a smile on his face using black food coloring and a fine paintbrush.

5 Partially mix a tiny amount of black ready-to-roll fondant with a little white for his hair. Scrunch and tear the fondant into little bits and stick them to the sides of his head. Make a little cap by rolling ¼ oz of white fondant into a thick disk shape. Pinch and pull the fondant on one side to form a peak. Stick this on his head. Finish off the head by sticking two tiny balls of flesh-colored fondant either side of the head for his ears. Add a little detail by making a small dent in each one with the end of a paintbrush.

6 Roll two ¼-oz lumps of black rolled fondant into two oval shapes for his feet and stick one on the end of each leg.

7 To make the paint pot, roll ¼ oz of gray ready-to-roll fondant into a stumpy cylindrical shape. Press a piping nozzle or something similar into the side to leave a semi-circular impression for the handle. Place the pot between his legs.

For the paintbrush, make two tiny oblongs of brown ready-to-roll fondant and one of black. Stick them together like an upside-down "T" shape and press lines into the black one with a knife to make bristles. Place the brush just in front of the handyman's left arm. Use two small flattened balls of flesh-colored fondant for his hands and stick these as though he is holding the paint pot and brush.

8 To make the planks of wood, roll 3½ oz dark brown fondant and ¾ oz white together into a sausage. Fold the sausage in half and roll again. Keep rolling and folding to achieve a woodgrain effect. Roll out the fondant and cut out strips of varying lengths *(fig 2)*. Stick a few on and around the cake.

9 To make the rolls of wallpaper, partially knead 2 oz of blue ready-to-roll fondant and ¾ oz of white together to achieve a marbled effect. Carefully roll the fondant out and cut out two strips. Roll one strip up completely and the other about halfway. Stick them onto the cake.

Finally, dab splotches of black food coloring around the cake and on the character himself.

# Wild animals

My nephew Jack helped with the colors of this cake. *"Potamusses are gray,"* he informed me gravely, but to balance the cake, they had to be brown. However Jack pointed out, *"That's why they're in the water — because they're all covered in mud!"*

1   Shape the cake by cutting bits off the top to leave an irregular surface. Try to leave a flattish area towards the front of the cake for the "lake." Spread some of the cut-away pieces of cake with butter cream and build up a small hill behind the lake *(fig 1)*.

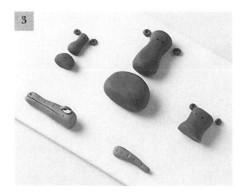

2   Place the cake on the cake board, slice and fill the center with butter cream. Reassemble the cake and spread a covering of butter cream over the sides and top. Keep any leftover butter cream if you are going to use this for the lake and greenery instead of classic fondant icing. Sprinkle the work surface with confectioner's sugar and knead 1 lb 2 oz white ready-to-roll fondant until pliable. Roll out the ready-to-roll fondant, then lift and place it over the cake. Carefully smooth the fondant into position.

3   To make life easier, construct the elephants, hippos and crocodile away from the cake and place in position later. For the elephants, first roll out ¼ oz gray ready-to-roll fondant to a thickness of about ⅜ in and cut out two disks. Make four small vertical cuts at quarter intervals around the edge of each disk for legs *(fig 2)*. Roll two 1½ oz lumps of gray fondant into two balls

for the bodies. Press gently on the front of each ball to make a slope to rest the head. Stick one ball onto each set of legs, making sure that both the slope and one of the small cuts are facing forward.

4   To make the heads, roll two ¾ oz lumps of gray fondant into chunky tennis racquet shapes. Stick one onto each body. Add nostrils by pushing the end of a paint-brush twice into the end of each trunk. Also press a couple of lines across each trunk with the back of a knife. To make the ears, roll about ⅛ oz of gray fondant into a ball. Flatten the ball and cut in half. Moisten the sides of the elephant's head and stick the ears in position. Repeat for the other elephant.
     To make a tail, roll a tiny ball of gray fondant into a thin string and stick it onto the rear of the elephant. Finally, stick two tiny disks of white ready-to-roll fondant on each face for eyes. Paint in the pupils and eyebrows with black food coloring.

5   To make the biggest hippo, roll 1 oz brown ready-to-roll fondant into a semi-circular shape for his body *(fig 3)*. Add a head by

rolling ¼ oz brown fondant into an oval. Squeeze the center of the oval slightly and stick onto the body. Stick two tiny brown balls onto the sides of the head for ears and add detail to each one by making a small hollow with the end of a paintbrush. Paint two tiny dots of black food coloring for the eyes. Make a smaller version for the baby.
     To make the submerged hippo, simply roll ¼ oz brown fondant into an oval and flatten the base so it can stand upright. Add ears and eyes.

## ■ INGREDIENTS

*   8-in round sponge cake (see pages 94-97)
*   1 quantity butter cream (see page 98)
*   Confectioner's sugar for rolling out
*   1 lb 8½ oz white ready-to-roll fondant
*   5¼ oz gray ready-to-roll fondant
*   Black food coloring
*   3½ oz brown ready-to-roll fondant
*   ½ oz green ready-to-roll fondant
*   Dark brown, gooseberry green and ice blue (or similar) food color pastes
*   3 tbsp white classic fondant icing (optional)
*   1 oz black ready-to-roll fondant

## ■ UTENSILS

*   Carving knife
*   10-in round cake board
*   Rolling pin
*   Small sharp knife
*   Water and paintbrush
*   Drinking straw
*   Piping nozzle
*   Large brush or pastry brush
*   Piping bag
*   Scissors

6 For the crocodile, roll ¼ oz green ready-to-–roll fondant into a sausage about 2½ in long. Try to make the ends slightly thicker than the middle *(fig 3)*. Press a line around the base of the sausage to make a mouth, and add scales by pressing a drinking straw held at an angle into the fondant. Also poke two dents for nostrils using the end of a paintbrush.

7 To make his eye, stick a tiny flattened oval of white fondant onto the side of the head and finish off with an eyebrow made from a tiny strip of green fondant bent into an "S" shape and stuck over the eye. Add a small dot of black food coloring for the pupil.

   To make the tail, roll the remaining green fondant into a long, tapering triangular shape and press a few scales into the sides, as on the head.

8 Using a fairly large paint- or pastry brush, paint the back of the cake using watered-down brown and green food coloring *(fig 4)*. (I used dark brown and gooseberry green food color pastes for this, but anything similar will do.) Place the elephants into position on the "grass" while it is still wet.

9 Partially mix a little blue food coloring into about 2 tbsp white classic fondant icing or butter cream if you prefer a softer finish. Swirl this over the front section of the top

of the cake and place the hippos and crocodile sections into position.

10 To make a monkey, roll ¼ oz brown ready-to-roll fondant into a cone *(fig 5)*. Stick this against the side of the cake and add a brown fondant ball on top for his head.

   For his features, make two tiny balls and an oval shape out of white ready-to-roll fondant. Flatten all three shapes and stick the two white disks on top of the head for his eyes and the oval just below for his

muzzle. Press the edge of a piping nozzle or something similar into the muzzle to make a smiling impression and paint three dots for the eyes and the nose with black food coloring. Stick two tiny balls of brown fondant either side of the head for his ears and make a small hollow into each one with the end of a paintbrush.

   For the arms, make two small sausages of brown fondant and stick these in whatever position you wish. Make another monkey for the other side of the cake.

11 To make the rocks, take 6 oz white fondant and 1 oz of black. Partially knead the two lumps together *(fig 6)*. Pull off small irregular lumps and stick these around the base of the cake and a few on top.

12 Color about 1 tbsp of classic fondant icing or butter cream green. Place the colored icing into a piping bag and secure the end. Snip about ⅛ in off the pointed end of the bag and pipe a few strands of foliage around the rocks on the sides and top of the cake *(fig 7)*.

**TIP**

*If you're really short of time but still want to make a cake in this style, raid your local candy shop or the confectionery counter at a large supermarket for jelly animal candies. Either substitute these for the modeled animals or add to the animals in the scene.*

# D e c o r a t i n g    v a r i a t i o n

In this simplified version, the basic cake was covered in the same way as the Baby cake on page 50. The animals were modeled as above, then surrounded by simple jungle-type leaves made from several shades of green ready-to-roll fondant. Details for making these are given in the Sunbather cake on page 82.

# Birthday fairy

*Here's someone who should brighten up any girl's birthday. If you want to cheat, your local cake-decorating shop should stock plastic figures made for inserting into cakes, although they may not have as much personality as this one!*

■ **INGREDIENTS**

- 1 pudding bowl cake (see page 94)
- ½ quantity butter cream (see page 98)
- Confectioner's sugar for rolling out
- 14 oz white ready-to-roll fondant
- 3 candy sticks (or candy cigarettes as they used to be known)
- ¾ oz flesh-colored ready-to-roll fondant
- Black food color paste
- ¾ oz yellow ready-to-roll fondant
- 9 oz pink ready-to-roll fondant
- 12 edible silver balls
- 1 sheet rice paper

■ **UTENSILS**

- Carving knife
- 8-in round cake board
- Cake spatula
- Rolling pin
- Small sharp knife
- Water and paintbrush
- Pencil
- Scissors

1 Level the top of the cake and place upside down in the center of the cake board. Slice and fill the center with a layer of butter cream and then spread a thin coating of butter cream over the top and sides of the cake.

2 Dust the work surface with confectioner's sugar. Knead and roll out 9 oz white ready-to-roll fondant. Carefully lift the fondant over the cake. Smooth the top and sides and neaten the base.

3 Stick one candy stick into the top of the cake to provide internal support for the fairy and roll 2 oz white fondant into an oval shape to form her body.

Gently squeeze the center to make a waist. Lightly moisten a small area on the top of the cake around the protruding candy stick and carefully slot the body into position (*fig 1*).

4 Insert a second candy stick into the top of the body leaving about 1¼ in poking out of the top.

Make a ¼-oz ball of flesh-colored fondant for her head and slot this onto the candy stick. Paint her features using black food coloring and a fine paintbrush. You can paint the head before putting it on her body, but be careful not to squash the face when lifting it. Add a tiny dot of fondant for a nose.

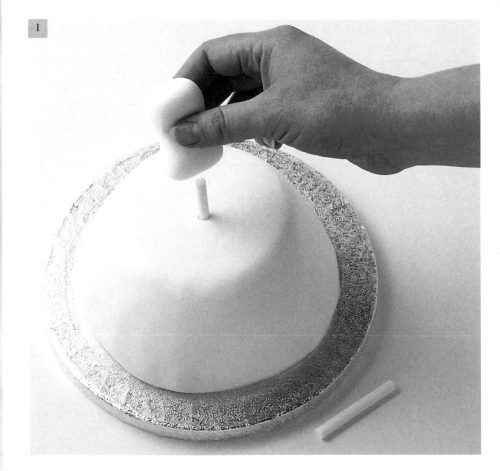

5 To make her hair, roll ⅛ oz of yellow ready-to-roll fondant into a strip about 3½ in x ¾ in (*fig 2*). Press lines down the length of the strip using the back of a knife. Stick the strip over her head and tweak the ends upwards to make them look like curls.

For the headdress make six tiny balls of pink ready-to-roll fondant. Stick three in a line on the top of her head with a little water. Stick another two above these and a final one on top.

Finish off her hair by cutting a tiny leaf shape out of some leftover yellow fondant. Press marks into it as you did for the other hair section, then stick this onto the front of her head.

6 Roll out 2 oz pink fondant and cut out a strip approximately 18 in x 1½ in. Making sure that the work surface is well dusted with confectioner's sugar so that the fondant doesn't stick, roll the paintbrush backwards and forwards along a small section of the strip at a time and a wonderful frill will develop (*fig 3*). Paint a line of water just above the base of the cake and, starting from the back of the fairy,

hands are holding the fairy wand.

Roll out the leftover yellow fondant and cut out a small star shape. Stick this onto the top of the wand with a little drop of water – not too much or the star will start to slide. You should also find that you are able to rest the star slightly against the fairy's body, which will provide it with some additional support.

9  Make a curved row of 12 small dents on the top frill of the fairy's dress using the end of a paintbrush. Put a tiny dab of water in each hollow and then add an edible silver ball as decoration.

10  To make her wings, place the rice paper over the wing template shown on page 109. Trace over it using a pencil. To make the second wing, turn the rice paper over and trace over it the other way. Cut out both wings, cutting just inside the pencil outline to avoid gray edges on the wings.

Take a small lump of white ready-to-roll fondant and moisten it with a drop of water

so that it becomes slightly tacky. Stick this onto the fairy's back and then carefully insert the two wings. Alternatively, you could stick them into position with a little dab of butter cream.

**TIP**

*If you cannot find any candy sticks in your local supermarket, you can use a lollipop stick instead to provide support inside the body and to act as a handle for the wand. Do remember, though, when cutting the cake, to remove the stick first and not to serve it to your guests!*

carefully stick the frill into place. If it breaks, simply cut off the straggly torn edge and continue with the rest of the frill.

Once you have gone all the way around, repeat the above procedure using about 1¾ oz white fondant to make a white frill. Stick this above the pink so that it overlaps slightly.

Continue up the skirt, alternating pink and white frills right up to the fairy's waist. Each frill will be about 2 in shorter than the last. Try to keep all the joins at the back.

7  Make a ribbon to hide the joins by thinly rolling out ¾ oz pink ready-to-roll fondant. Cut out two thin strips for the tails of the ribbon *(fig 3)*. Cut a "V" shape into the end of each one and stick them so that they fall down the back of the skirt.

Top with a "bow" made of two tiny pink triangles and a small flattened ball of pink for the knot itself. As this detail is not visible from the front of the cake, you could always leave out this stage if you're a bit short of time.

8  Press and stick the remaining candy stick against the fairy's body using a little water. This will form the handle of the wand. Roll ¼ oz flesh-colored ready-to-roll fondant into a sausage. Cut this in half for the arms. Flatten one end of each sausage slightly to make her hands, then carefully stick these against the side of the figure to look as though the

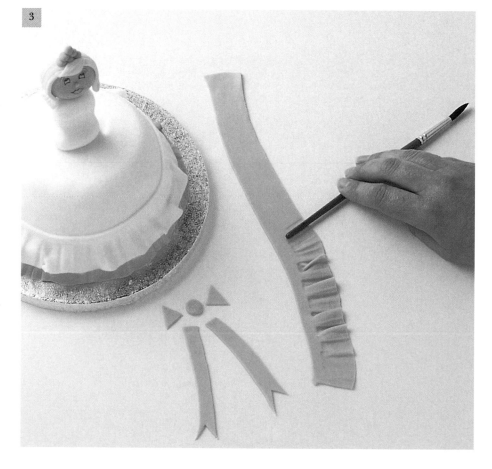

# Christmas Santas

*Ideal for anyone who loves the nuts and almond paste that abound around Christmas-time, this is an extremely easy cake to decorate. Try to use white almond paste rather than yellow, as this takes the colors better.*

1 Follow the fruitcake recipe for an 8-inch round cake on page 95 to the point where you have spooned the mixture into the baking pan. Before placing it in the oven, arrange a selection of nuts over the top of the mixture. Use your favorite nuts or whatever you have in your cupboard and start from the outside of the cake and work in. I began with a circle of almonds, then a line of pecans. Next came a circle of filberts, some nice big chunky brazil nuts and finally half a walnut in the center.

Trim a piece of waxed paper to fit over the top of the pan and cut a small hole about 1¼ in out of the center. Rest this over the cake before baking to stop the nuts browning too much during the cooking process. If you have a fan oven, use a sheet of waxed paper long enough to tuck under the baking pan, otherwise it will simply fly off as soon as you shut the door.

Bake as normal, removing the waxed paper about ten minutes before the end of the cooking time just to lightly brown and color the nuts.

■ INGREDIENTS

• 8-inch round fruitcake (See page 95 and read step 1 before baking.)
• Selection of nuts, such as almonds, pecans, filberts, walnuts, etc.
• 3 tbsp brandy (optional)
• 4 tbsp apricot jam
• Confectioner's sugar for rolling out
• Red, paprika, dark brown and green food color pastes
• 1 lb 9¼ oz white (neutral) almond paste, divided and colored as follows:
  8¼ oz red
  5 oz flesh color (paprika)
  4 oz dark brown
  1 oz green
  Leave the remaining almond paste white (neutral).

■ UTENSILS

• Waxed paper
• 9-inch round cake board
• Toothpick
• Strainer
• Pastry brush
• Rolling pin
• Small sharp knife
• Water and paintbrush

2 When the cake has cooled, turn it out of the pan and place onto a 9-inch round cake board.

For an extra festive touch, pierce the cake a few times between the nuts with a toothpick (you can lift a few of the nuts up if you wish) and carefully drizzle about 2 tbsp brandy over the cake. Allow it to seep in and replace any nuts you might have moved.

Boil the apricot jam either in a saucepan or in a non-metallic dish in a microwave for about one minute. Strain the jam to remove any lumps of fruit and mix in the last remaining tablespoon of brandy. (You may omit the brandy if you prefer.) Paint the mixture over the top and sides of the cake using a pastry brush to give it a wonderfully gleaming finish (*fig 1*).

3 To make the 12 figures, begin with the bodies. Sprinkle your work surface with confectioner's sugar. Take a ½-oz piece of red-colored almond paste and roll it into a flattish conical shape. Press

2

and stick the body up against the side of the cake. You shouldn't need any water to keep it in place – the jam around the sides should be adequate to hold it.

Make another identical body and stick this directly opposite. Stick the third and fourth bodies halfway between the first two (*fig 2*). The cake should now be divided into quarters. Make and stick another two bodies between each of the four Santas already in position, leaving a small space between each one for his sack. Continue until all the bodies are evenly spaced around the side of the cake.

4  To make a head, roll a ¼-oz ball of flesh-colored almond paste into an oval shape (*fig 3*). Stick this on top of one of the bodies already in position. Repeat on the other eleven Santas.

5  For each hat, form ⅛ oz of red almond paste into a small triangular shape. Tweak the end into a point and bend it over slightly. Place it on one of the heads. The tip of the hat should rest just on top of the cake. Repeat and make hats for all the other figures, insuring that they all point in the same direction.

6  To make the beards, thinly roll out ¼ oz of uncolored (white) almond paste. Press lines into the almond paste using the back

of a knife and cut out a triangular shape. Stick this onto Santa's face so that the beard hangs over the front of the body. If it won't stay in place, use a little water.

Push the end of a paintbrush into the beard to leave behind a surprised, open-mouthed expression. Stick on a tiny ball of flesh-colored almond paste for Santa's nose. Repeat on each Santa.

7  To decorate a hat, take about ⅛ oz white almond paste. Pull off a tiny piece and roll it into a ball for the pom-pom. Stick in place. Roll the rest into a sausage and lay it around the brim of the hat so that it almost obscures all the face. Repeat on the rest of the hats.

8  Use ¼ oz brown almond paste for each sack and shape into a cone. Stand each one on its fattest part, then pinch and pull the almond paste at the top to make a neck (*fig 3*). Press one between each Santa on the side of the cake.

9  To make the presents, roll out 1 oz green almond paste to a thickness of about ⅜ in. Cut out twelve tiny green squares. Using the back of a knife, make a crisscross pattern on the front of each parcel. Place one in the top of each sack and bend the neck of the sack up slightly. Brush away any dusty confectioner's sugar marks using a damp paintbrush.

**TIP**

*If the almond paste is too hard for you to knead properly, soften it for just a few seconds on high in the microwave.*

3

# Weary windsurfer

*This cake was made for a keen windsurfing friend. If you don't feel up to painting, make the pool from one solid color or stick spots or other sugar paste shapes around the side.*

1 Begin by making the surfboard. Roll out 1 ¾ oz white ready-to-roll fondant on a surface dusted with confectioner's sugar and cut out a board shape, using the template if necessary. Place the board somewhere out of the way to harden slightly while you assemble the rest of the cake.

2 Level the top of the cake if necessary and turn it upside down. Slice and fill the middle of the cake with butter cream. Reassemble and place the cake in the center of the cake board. Spread a thin layer of butter cream over the top and sides, saving some if using butter cream for the water.

3 Sprinkle the work surface with confectioner's sugar and roll out and cover the cake with the rest of the white ready-to-roll fondant. Smooth over the top and sides and trim away any excess from the base.

4 Begin constructing the windsurfer by building a life jacket. Shape the orange ready-to-roll fondant into a thick "U" shape and press three vertical lines down the

length of the jacket using the back of a knife (*fig 1*). Stick this onto the cake. Roll ¾ oz of flesh-colored ready-to-roll fondant into a ball for his head and stick in position. Paint in the eyes using black food coloring and a fine paintbrush and stick three tiny balls of flesh-colored fondant on the face for his ears and nose. To add detail, poke the end of a paintbrush into each ear to leave a little hollow.

5 Take about half a teaspoon of classic fondant icing or butter cream and mix in a little brown food coloring. (A nice touch here would be to color the hair the same shade as the recipient's.) Using a knife, smear the hair on top of the head and pull it up slightly to give it a bit of texture.
  Roll ⅛ oz flesh-colored fondant into a sausage for one of the arms. Flatten one end slightly to make a hand and stick the arm against the side of the body, bending it at the elbow so that the hand covers the mouth area.

6 For the water, partially mix a little blue food coloring into about 2 tbsp classic fondant icing or butter cream. Spread around the windsurfer on top of the cake (*fig 2*).

7 Roll the dark blue fondant into a sausage about 18 inches long. Starting from the back of the cake, lay this around the top edge. Neaten and stick the join together. Place the surfboard in position so that the tip just rests on the edge of the pool. Make two flattish oval shapes from flesh-colored fondant for his feet and insert these into the water. Make the other arm, squashing one end slightly to make a hand, and stick this in place with the palm just resting on the board.

8 Cut a triangle out of thin cardboard and stick this to the candy stick with a little classic fondant icing or butter cream. Insert this into the top of the cake.

## INGREDIENTS

- Confectioner's sugar for rolling out
- 10½ oz white ready-to-roll fondant
- 6-inch round cake (see pages 94-97)
- ½ quantity butter cream (see page 98)
- 2 tbsp classic fondant icing (optional)
- 2 oz orange ready-to-roll fondant
- 1¾ oz flesh-colored ready-to-roll fondant
- Assorted food paste colors for painting, including black and brown
- 2 oz dark blue ready-to-roll fondant
- 1 candy stick (candy cigarette)
- 1 oz green-colored sugar (see page 98)

## UTENSILS

- Rolling pin
- Small sharp knife
- Surfboard template (see page 109)
- Carving knife
- Cake spatula
- Water
- Medium and fine paintbrushes
- Thin cardboard triangle for sail
- Clean damp cloth

9 Paint a design on the sides of the pool. Start by painting the colors first and add the outlines in black food coloring afterwards. If you do it the other way round, the black will bleed into the color. If you make a mistake, wash over the area with fresh water and wipe away the mistake with a clean, damp cloth.

10 Moisten the exposed cake board with a little water and carefully spoon the colored sugar around the base to cover the rest of the board.

# Spotted dog

*This chap just goes to prove that Man's best friend is his cake! If you're feeling adventurous, why not adapt him to look like the family pet. To make a hairy version, cover him with chocolate butter cream and "rough it up" with a fork.*

■ **INGREDIENTS**
- Confectioner's sugar for rolling out
- 10½ oz green ready-to-roll fondant (see page 98)
- 1 pudding bowl cake (see page 94)
- 1 quantity butter cream (see page 98)
- 1 lb 12 oz white ready-to-roll fondant
- 10½ oz black ready-to-roll fondant
- ¾ oz red ready-to-roll fondant
- 1¾ oz flesh-colored ready-to-roll fondant
- Candies for decoration

■ **UTENSILS**
- Water and paintbrush
- 12-in round cake board
- Rolling pin
- Carving knife
- Small sharp knife
- Cooking spatula
- Wooden spoon

1 Begin by covering the cake board. Lightly moisten the board with a little water and place to one side. Sprinkle the work surface with confectioner's sugar and begin to roll out the green ready-to-roll fondant. Carefully lift the fondant and place it on the cake board. Continue to roll right to the edges of the cake board. Trim and neaten the edges and place the board to one side again.

2 On a spare cake board, cutting board or work surface, check that the cake will lie flat when it is turned upside down. Slice a little off the base if necessary. Cut the cake in half, and fill the middle with a layer of butter cream. Spread a thin coating of butter cream around the sides and top of the cake as well.

   Knead and roll out 10½ oz white ready-to-roll fondant. Lift and place the fondant over the cake and carefully smooth it into position. Trim and neaten around the base. Lift the cake using a spatula to help avoid getting fingerprints in the fondant and place it towards the back of the covered cake board.

3 To make the dog's head, take 7 oz white ready-to-roll fondant and roll this into a ball. Flatten the ball slightly into a thick disk about 4½ in wide and stick this to the front of the cake.

4 To make the dog's eyes, thinly roll out about ¾ oz black ready-to-roll fondant. Cut out two disks about 1¾ in wide and two about 1 in in diameter.

   Wipe your hands (black fondant has an annoying tendency to get everywhere!) and roll out about ¼ oz white ready-to-roll fondant. Cut out two disks each about 1¼ in wide and squash two tiny balls of white to make the tiny disks for the highlights. Assemble and stick the eyes in position on the face starting with the largest black disk first and alternating the colors.

5 For the tongue, use ¾ oz red ready-to-roll fondant. Roll this into a sort of flattish, carrot shape and bend it into a slight curve. Press a line down the center using the back of a knife and stick it into position on the board, the pointed end just touching the base of the face.

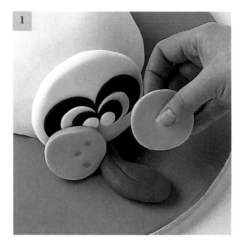

6 To make the dog's muzzle, divide the flesh-colored ready-to-roll fondant in two and roll each half into a ball. Flatten each ball into a disk about 2 in in diameter. Stick the two circles in place and make three small dents in each using the end of a wooden spoon (*fig 1*).

   Finish off the face by sticking a small ball of black fondant onto the muzzle for his nose.

7 To make the legs, divide 10½ oz white ready-to-roll fondant into four. Roll each quarter into a chunky carrot shape. Flatten each paw slightly and stick them on the board around the dog. Using the back of a knife, press three short lines into the front of each paw.

8 To make the ears, take 5 oz black ready-to-roll fondant. Divide it into two pieces and roll each half into the same sort of carrot shape as you did for the legs.

Use a rolling pin to flatten each half into an ear shape. Stick one either side of the head (*fig 2*).

9 Roll out 3½ oz of black ready-to-roll fondant and cut out splotches in a variety of shapes and sizes. Stick these all over the dog's back. Make a tail by rolling ¼ oz black ready-to-roll fondant into a tapering sausage shape. Bend it into a curl and stick in position.

10 Decorate the cake board with a selection of small candies, securing them in place with little dabs of butter cream.

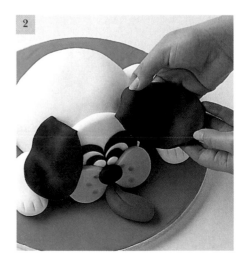

# Soccer fan

*Although the theme of this cake is soccer, it could be adapted to suit other sports. Substitute a brown rolled fondant ball and you have a basketball cake. Substitute a bat, long pants and a cap — it's baseball!*

### ■ INGREDIENTS

- 6-in square sponge cake (see pages 94-97)
- 1 quantity butter cream (see page 98)
- Confectioner's sugar for rolling out
- 12 oz green ready-to-roll fondant
- 10½ oz white ready-to-roll fondant
- 5 oz red ready-to-roll fondant
- ¾ oz black ready-to-roll fondant
- 1 oz flesh-colored ready-to-roll fondant
- 1¾ oz blue ready-to-roll fondant
- Black food coloring
- ⅛ oz brown ready-to-roll fondant
- 2 oz green-colored coconut (see page 98)

### ■ UTENSILS

- Carving knife
- 10-in square cake board
- Cake spatula
- Cake smoother (optional)
- Small sharp knife
- Water
- Medium and fine paintbrushes

1  Slice a little off the top of the cake to level it if necessary. Turn it upside down and place towards the back of the board. Slice and fill the middle of the cake with butter cream, then reassemble and spread a thin covering of butter cream over the top and sides.

2  Dust the work surface with a little confectioner's sugar and knead all the green ready-to-roll fondant until pliable. Roll it out, then lift and place over the cake. Smooth over the top and sides, preferably with a cake smoother, as this irons out any lumps and bumps. Alternatively, simply smooth it as best you can with the flat of your hand. Trim away any excess from around the base.

3  Make the scarf by rolling out 8 oz of the white ready-to-roll fondant and cutting it into a strip 12 in x 4 in. Moisten the top of the cake and carefully lay the scarf over the top.

   Roll out and cut 5 oz of red ready-to-roll fondant into about seven thin strips about 11 in x 4 in. Lay and stick the red stripes across the scarf. When you come to the ones at either end, cut a fringe into the strip before laying it into position on the board (*fig 1*).

4  Begin with the soccer fan's feet. Divide the black ready-to-roll fondant in two and roll each half into an oval. Stick these onto the board in front of the cake. Make two socks

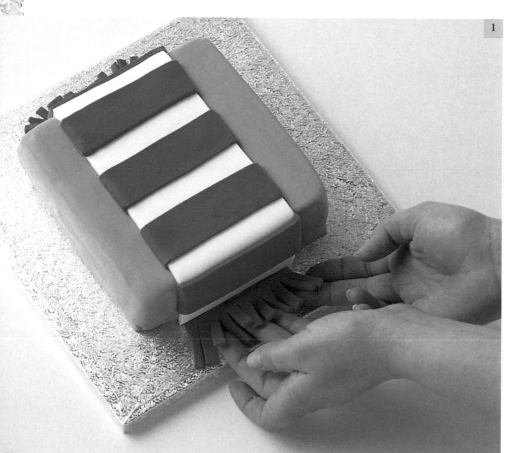

by rolling ¼ oz white ready-to-roll fondant into two balls. Flatten each ball slightly and press a few horizontal lines into each sock with the back of a knife. Stick these onto the boots (*fig 2*).

   Make the soccer fan's legs by rolling ¼ oz flesh-colored ready-to-roll fondant into a thin string. Cut this in half and stick into position.

5  For his shorts, take ¼ oz white ready-to-roll fondant and roll it into a boomerang shape (*fig 3*). Stick on top of the cake. Pull off and keep a little bit of the blue ready-to-roll fondant to make the sleeves later. Roll the rest into a cone for his body and stick on

> ### TIP
> *If the soccer fan loses his head or falls over, insert a small strand of dried spaghetti inside the body and slot the head on top for extra support.*

3

small dent in them with the end of a paintbrush.

Paint in the pupils, eyebrows and mouth with black food coloring. Finally, roll a little brown fondant into a tiny strip and place on top of the head, Press some lines into the hair with the back of a knife.

9   Moisten the top of the cake and any exposed cake board with a little water and then sprinkle with the green-colored coconut to look like the grass of a soccer field.

**TIP**

*If you know the home colors of the recipient's favorite team, make the scarf and the fan's clothes in the appropriate shades.*

top of the shorts (*fig 2*). Flatten the top of the cone slightly so the head has a level surface to sit on.

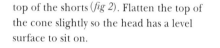

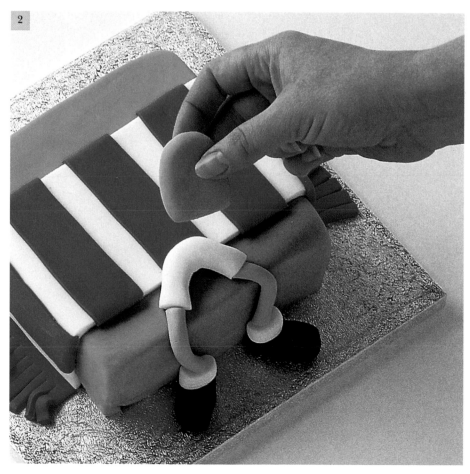

2

6   For the ball, roll ¾ oz white ready-to-roll fondant into a ball. Stick this in place and paint a hexagonal design on the front with black food coloring and a fine paintbrush. (If you don't want to paint, just press a few lines into the ball with the back of a knife or leave it plain.)

7   Roll ⅛ oz flesh-colored ready-to-roll fondant into a thin sausage to make his arms. Cut in two and flatten one end of each half to make the hands. Stick these into position.

Make two tiny shirt sleeves by rolling the leftover blue fondant into an oval. Cut in half and stick one on the top of each arm.

8   To make the head, roll ¼ oz flesh-colored ready-to-roll fondant into a ball. Stick on top of the body.

Stick two tiny flattened disks of white ready-to-roll fondant onto the face for his eyes and three small balls of flesh-colored fondant in position for his ears and nose. Add some detail to the ears by making a

# Makeup bag

*This is for anyone who likes to experiment with the latest cosmetics. It is also very adaptable. Make a brown bag and fill with fondant toys for a Christmas sack or pack with fondant pencils and books for a "Back to School" cake.*

## ■ INGREDIENTS

- Confectioner's sugar for rolling out
- 2 oz gray ready-to-roll fondant (see page 98)
- 1 oz dark brown ready-to-roll fondant
- ¾ oz flesh-colored ready-to-roll fondant
- 2 oz light brown ready-to-roll fondant
- 4¼ oz black ready-to-roll fondant
- ¾ oz dark blue ready-to-roll fondant
- ¼ oz light blue ready-to-roll fondant
- 1 lb 9 oz white ready-to-roll fondant
- ¾ oz red ready-to-roll fondant
- 4¼ oz pink ready-to-roll fondant
- ¼ oz pale green ready-to-roll fondant
- 6-in round sponge cake (see pages 94-97)
- ½ quantity butter cream (see page 98)

## ■ UTENSILS

- Rolling pin
- Small sharp knife
- Water and paintbrush
- Carving knife
- Cake spatula
- 9-in round cake board
- Ruler

1 Begin by making up the little cosmetics themselves *(fig 1)* and, if possible, leave them overnight to harden. This will give them the strength to stand up and look even more realistic. If the recipient has a particular penchant for any specific brand of makeup or perfume, it might be fun to try to copy the bottles or packaging to give the cake a really personal touch.

Dust the work surface with confectioner's sugar. To make a basic eyeshadow palette, roll out about ¾ oz gray ready-to-roll fondant. Roll it fairly thickly and cut out a semi-circle. Roll out three small lumps of fondant in various shades of brown and paprika and cut a different section of a smaller semi-circle out of each. Stick these onto the gray.

2 To make a duo eyeshadow, roll and cut about ¼ oz black ready-to-roll fondant into a rectangle. Cut two smaller rectangles out of two different shades of blue fondant and stick these onto the black. Make an applicator wand by rolling a little light brown ready-to-roll fondant into a thin string and sticking a tiny oval of white or cream fondant on either end.

3 To make a lipstick, roll about ¼ oz gray ready-to-roll fondant into a thick sausage. Slice a little off both ends to neaten them and press two lines across the fondant using the back of a knife. Make another smaller sausage out of pink, red or whatever shade of ready-to-roll fondant you like and slice a small section to flatten one of the ends. Make a diagonal cut through the other end to make an authentic lipstick shape and stick the two sections together. Make another two or three of these.

To make a lip pencil, roll about ¼ oz red ready-to-roll fondant into a sausage about 3½ in long. Slice a little off both ends to neaten them. Roll a small piece of flesh-colored ready-to-roll fondant into a tiny cone and slice a little off the pointed end.

Make a tiny red point and stick all three sections together. Make a couple of eye pencils in exactly the same way using blue and brown fondants.

4 For the blusher brush, roll about ¾ oz light brown ready-to-roll fondant into a sausage. Slice off both ends to neaten them. Roll a little gray fondant into a ball. Flatten the ball slightly and stick this against the brown. Press two lines into the gray with the back of a knife to add detail.

Roll out about ¼ oz black ready-to-roll fondant to a thickness of about ⅜ in. Cut this into a triangular shape with a flat top and make bristles by pressing lines down the length of the shape with a knife. Stick the "brush" in place on the handle.

1

5   Make a simple pot of cream by rolling about 2 oz white ready-to-roll fondant into a round cylindrical shape with a flat base and top. Roll ¾ oz pink fondant into a thick disk and stick this on top of the pot. Press a few vertical lines around the edge of the lid. Make a smaller pot out of two shades of brown ready-to-roll fondant to sit on the board.

6   To make a tube, roll about ¾ oz white fondant into a slightly tapering rectangular shape. Make a small flowerpot shape out of a little white fondant and stick this onto the end of the tube for a lid. Press lines down the length of the lid using the back of a knife.

7   For the mascara wand, simply roll about ¼ oz pale green ready-to-roll fondant into a sausage. Neaten both ends and press two lines into the fondant about a third of the way along the top of the shape.
    Make any additional cosmetics and place all the components to one side while you deal with the cake.

8   Slice and fill the middle of the cake with butter cream. Reassemble the cake and place it in the center of the board. Spread a thin covering of butter cream over the top and sides.
    Roll out 3½ oz black ready-to-roll fondant and cut out a 6-in disk and place on top of the cake. You could use your baking pan as a template for this, but accuracy is not vitally important here as most of it will be hidden. The reason for the black is simply to help seal in the cake beneath and to give the illusion that the bag is full, should you have any gaps between your components. Place the pink-and-white pot and the white tube of cream on top of the black.

9   Take 10½ oz white ready-to-roll fondant and 3½ oz of pink. Partially knead the two

**TIP**

*For a really quick cake with no modeling, simply fill the top of the cake with candies or cookies instead.*

colors together to achieve a light marbled effect. Roll the fondant out fairly thick and cut out a strip about 18 in x 6 in. Using the edge of a clean ruler, gently press a crisscross pattern across the strip to give a quilted effect (*fig 2*).

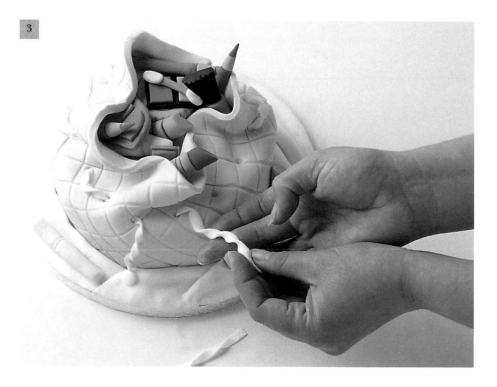

10  Carefully wind the strip up loosely like a bandage and, holding it vertically, start at the back and unwind it around the side of the cake (see page 38). Neaten the join and base. If it looks a bit flat in places, insert a few lumps of fondant to pad out the top of the bag slightly. Using the end of a paintbrush, make a line of circular dents around the side of the bag. Carefully place the cosmetics into the top of the bag and secure with a little water.

11  Moisten the exposed cake board. Thinly roll out 9 oz white ready-to-roll fondant into a long strip. Lay the strip around the base of the cake, allowing it to fall into folds like fabric. Press down the fondant at the edges of the board and trim away any excess. Place any leftover cosmetics around the board.

12  Thinly roll out ¾ oz white fondant and cut into small thin strips. Take one strip and twist it (*fig 3*). Hang it between two of the holes around the side of the cake and secure the ends with a little water. Repeat using alternate holes to look like a cord threaded through the fondant. When you come to the final two at the front of the cake, allow them to hang down. Finish off each one with a tiny ball of white fondant.

# Lovebirds

*Here's a novel idea for an engagement cake without a pink sugar heart in sight! It would also make a loving gift for Valentine's day. This is an extremely easy cake to put together as the chocolate sticks hide a multitude of sins!*

## ■ INGREDIENTS

- Confectioner's sugar for rolling out
- 4 oz pale blue ready-to-roll fondant
- ¼ oz white ready-to-roll fondant
- Black food coloring
- 1 pudding bowl cake (see page 94)
- ½ quantity chocolate butter cream (see page 98)
- Two 4-oz boxes of chocolate sticks (flavor of your choice!)
- 2 oz dark blue ready-to-roll fondant
- 1 oz green ready-to-roll fondant

## ■ UTENSILS

- Water
- Fine and medium paintbrushes
- Rolling pin
- Piping nozzle
- Small sharp knife
- Carving knife
- 8-in round cake board
- Cake spatula
- Template for tail (see page 109)
- Scalloped cutter or garrett frill

1

1   Roll two 2 oz lumps of pale blue ready-to-roll fondant into two conical shapes for the birds' bodies. Check that the bases are flat enough for them to stand upright. Make two 1-oz balls of pale blue fondant for the heads *(fig 1)*. Stick a head onto each body with a little water.

2   To make the eyes, thinly roll out about ¼ oz white ready-to-roll fondant. Cut out four small circles using a piping nozzle and stick two on each head. Paint pupils and eyelashes using black food coloring. Make two tiny yellow fondant triangles for the beaks. Press a line using the back of a knife into the sides of each beak and stick one on each bird. Make a tiny pale blue triangle and press a few lines into the front of it. Stick it on top of the male bird's head. Put the birds to one side.

3   Level the top of the cake if necessary and slice and fill the center with butter cream. Reassemble the cake and dab a little butter cream in the center of the cake board to help hold the cake in place. Stand the cake,

widest part up, and spread a thick layer of butter cream all over the sides and top.

4   Place the two birds into position on top of the cake and begin to build up the nest. Do this by pressing the chocolate sticks, one at a time, around the sides of the nest *(fig 2)* and over the top edge.

2

5   Roll out 1 oz of the dark blue ready-to-roll fondant and cut out a tail using the template on page 109 if necessary. Re-knead the leftover fondant and cut out a second tail. Place the two tails in position, one behind each bird.

6   To make the birds' wings, roll out another 1 oz dark blue ready-to-roll fondant and using either a scalloped cutter or a garrett frill, cut out a frilly circle. Re-knead the fondant and cut out a second circle of the same size. Cut both circles in half. Carefully stick two wings onto each of the birds, overlapping them slightly at the front as though they are holding hands (sorry — wings!) *(fig 3)*.

7   Roll out the green fondant and cut out some simple leaves. Press a couple of veins into each leaf using the back of a knife and stick the leaves around the board and against the cake with a little water.

3

# Woodland creatures

*These little people should appeal to both children and adults who have never really grown up, bringing special birthday magic to any party. Alternatively, select some of the woodland animals shown in the picture overleaf as decoration.*

1 Level the top of the cake and turn it upside down. Slice the cake in two and fill the center with butter cream. Place on the board and spread more butter cream around the sides and top.

2 Knead and roll out 11 oz of the white almond paste. Place either a 7-in round cake board or plate on top to act as a template and cut around it using a sharp knife. Place the almond paste disk on top of the cake.

3 Roll out the remaining almond paste and cut a strip measuring approximately 23 in x 3 in. Carefully roll up the strip like a bandage, then unwind it around the side of the cake *(fig 1)*.

4 Press irregular vertical lines around the sides of the cake using the back of a knife.

### TIP
*Use the leaves as camouflage and position them to hide any mistakes or unsightly marks!*

Use a paintbrush to paint the bark with a wash of watered-down brown food coloring *(fig 2)*. Finally, paint a few "age" rings on top of the tree stump with brown food coloring and a fine paintbrush.

5 To make the troll, roll out 1 oz white ready-to-roll fondant into a cone *(fig 3)* to form the basis for his body. Stick this in position on top of the tree stump.

6 For the troll's legs, roll ¾ oz mint green ready-to-roll fondant into a sausage and cut this in half. Stick the two halves to the base of the body.

7 To make the arms, roll ¼ oz white ready-to-roll fondant into a sausage and cut in half, as done for the legs. Stick one arm either side of the body.

## ■ INGREDIENTS
- 7-in round sponge cake (see pages 94-97)
- I quantity butter cream (see page 98)
- Confectioner's sugar for rolling out
- 1 lb 12 oz white almond paste
- Dark brown food color paste
- 7 oz white ready-to-roll fondant
- 2 oz flesh-colored ready-to-roll fondant
- 4 oz mint green ready-to-roll fondant
- 2 oz gooseberry green ready-to-roll fondant
- 2 oz red ready-to-roll fondant
- ¾ oz black ready-to-roll fondant
- ¼ oz gray ready-to-roll fondant
- Black food color paste
- 3 oz dark brown sugar

## ■ UTENSILS
- II-in round cake board
- Carving knife
- Cake spatula
- Rolling pin
- 7-in round cake board or plate
- Small sharp knife
- Water
- Paintbrush

**3**

11 For each toadstool, roll out ¼ oz white ready-to-roll fondant into a cone *(fig 4)*. Make another three cones and stick them in position around the base of the cake. Divide 1 oz of the red fondant into two and roll into little balls. Cut each ball in half and stick one on top of each toadstool base. Decorate each one with a few tiny flattened disks of white fondant.

12 To make the snail, roll ¼ oz gray ready-to-roll fondant into a small sausage. Paint a line of water along the top. Roll it up, leaving about ¾ in protruding for the head *(fig 4)*.

   Pinch two tiny "feelers" out of the top of the head and paint three dots of black food coloring on the face for the eyes and mouth. Place the snail at the foot of the tree stump and secure with a little water.

13 For the leaves, take the two remaining shades of green-colored fondant and roll each one out flat. Cut out some very basic

**4**

dots of black food coloring on the face for his eyes.

10 Repeat steps 5-9 given above for the remaining trolls, although you can omit making legs for the one shown on the right of the cake as his lower body is strategically hidden by some of the leaves!

**TIP**

*If your almond paste is difficult to handle, soften it for a few seconds on high power in a microwave.*

8 Stick a small ball of flesh-colored ready-to-roll fondant on top of the body for the troll's head. For the hat, roll ¼ oz red fondant into a pointed triangular shape and stick on top of the head, tweaking the end out at an angle. Make three tiny balls of flesh-colored fondant. Use one for his nose and the other two as hands. Make two tiny flesh-colored triangles for ears. Stick these in place and add a little detail by pressing the end of a paintbrush lightly into each ear.

9 To complete the troll, make two small ovals of black fondant and stick one onto the end of each leg. Paint two tiny

**5**

leaf shapes using the tip of a knife. Press a simple vein pattern into each leaf using the back of the knife *(fig 5)*. Arrange around the scene.

14 Lightly moisten the exposed cake board and carefully spoon the dark brown sugar around the bottom of it to look like earth.

**TIP**
*Instead of sugar, you could substitute green-colored shredded coconut as grass. Together with quick-to-make details like the little snail, the area around the cake contributes to the overall "tableau," resulting in a totally professional finish.*

# Decorating variation

In this alternative version, I have used rabbits instead of figures. Instructions for making these appear on page 105 and the effect is just as charming as the original. Add some sugar eggs for an Easter theme. If your creativity is really flowing, you could also add mice, squirrels, or other small creatures. You could also devise a Christmas or winter scene. Spread a layer of classic fondant icing over the top of the tree stump and the group to look like snow and add beards and white trims to the hats of the figures.

# Santa and friends

*I do like cakes that tell a story. It means that people actually have to take some time to look at them to work out what's going on. Here, Santa and his helper are putting the finishing touches to some teddy bears ready for the big night.*

1  Although I have used a traditional fruitcake base here, you could substitute sponge if you prefer. Just omit the brandy, jam, and almond paste and use butter cream instead. To shape the cake, cut irregular lumps out of the cake and place these pieces around the cake to create the snowdrifts (*fig 1*). (You could leave the cake intact if you prefer.)

 If you wish, pierce the cake a few times with a cocktail stick and drizzle the brandy over the top. Place the cake on the board and "paint" with boiled apricot jam, applied with a pastry brush.

2  Dust the work surface with confectioner's sugar and knead the almond paste until pliable. (If it is difficult to knead, heat it for a few seconds in a microwave on full power.) Roll it out and cover the cake.

3  Lightly moisten the whole of the cake and the exposed cake board with a little water. Roll out 14 oz white ready-to-roll fondant. Lay this over the cake and board. Smooth the fondant over the cake and board, starting from the center to try to prevent air bubbles from forming in the hollows. Trim and neaten the edges.

 If you do get an air bubble, prick it gently with the toothpick and press out. Hide the little hole left by the toothpick under a figure or snowball later.

4  To make Santa, roll 1¼ oz red ready-to-roll fondant into a cone (*fig 2*). Stick this in the

## ■ INGREDIENTS

- 6-in square fruitcake
- 3 tbsp brandy (optional)
- 3 tbsp boiled apricot jelly
- Confectioner's sugar for rolling out
- 1 lb 2 oz almond paste
- 1 lb white ready-to-roll fondant
- 2 oz red ready-to-roll fondant
- 1 oz flesh-colored ready-to-roll fondant
- Black food coloring
- 1 oz golden brown ready-to-roll fondant
- 1 oz green ready-to-roll fondant

## ■ UTENSILS

- Carving knife
- Toothpick
- 8-in square cake board
- Pastry brush
- Rolling pin
- Small sharp knife
- Water
- Medium and fine paintbrushes
- Drinking straw

middle of the cake. Roll ¼ oz of flesh-colored fondant into a ball for his head and stick on the body.

 To make his beard, roll out about ⅛ oz white ready-to-roll fondant and cut out a triangular shape. Press lines into the beard with the back of a knife and stick onto the face. Stick a tiny ball of flesh-colored fondant just above the beard for his nose and two either side of the head for his ears. Push the end of a paintbrush into each ear to add detail.

 For the hat, roll ⅛ oz red ready-to-roll fondant into a triangle. Stick on top of the head and bend the end over slightly. Roll ⅛ oz white fondant into a thin sausage and lay this around the base of the hat. Stick a small ball of white on the end of the hat for a pom-pom. Paint two dots of black food coloring for his eyes.

5  Next, roll ¼ oz black ready-to-roll fondant into a sausage about 3 in long for his boots. Cut this in half and bend up the end of each to make an "L" shape. Stick in position, making sure that you leave enough room for the teddy bear later. Press a few lines into the sole of each boot with the back of a knife. Roll ¼ oz white ready-

1

mouth by pressing a drinking straw held at an angle to leave an upside-down, semicircular impression. Paint the pupils on these teddy bears as though they are looking to the right.

On the finished teddy bears add ears, and pupils looking to the left. Hold and press the drinking straw the other way up to give them smiling expressions.

8   To make the elf's body, roll ¼ oz green ready-to-roll fondant into a ball (*fig 3*). Stick towards the front of the cake. Roll ⅛ oz flesh-colored ready-to-roll fondant into a ball for his head and stick on the body.

Top the head with a small triangle of green fondant and tweak the end into position.

Make eyes in the same way as for the teddy bears and paint a smiling mouth using black food coloring. Make two tiny pointed ears and a nose, and stick in position on the head.

To make the legs, roll ⅛ oz green ready-to-roll fondant into a sausage. Cut in half and stick in position. Make a smaller sausage for the arms and stick these in place too. Make two tiny flesh-colored hands and make and place a teddy's ear in one. Stick in place.

Make two smaller versions of Santa's boots out of ⅛ oz black fondant and stick on the ends of the legs. Finally, roll any leftover bits of white fondant into balls and stick around the cake to look like snowballs.

**TIP**

*If you are very short of time, just make the one teddy bear that Santa is in the process of finishing off — the cake will look just as charming and will take you far less time. You could also leave out Santa's helper if you wish.*

to-roll fondant into a sausage about 7 in long. Lay this neatly around the base of the figure.

6   Make the first teddy bear. Roll ¼ oz of the brown ready-to-roll fondant into a cone (*fig 3*). Stick this in front of Santa. Roll ⅛ oz brown fondant into a ball for his head. Stick this on top of the body. Make two small sausage shapes for his legs and bend up the end of each one to make a foot. Stick one either side of the body. Stick two smaller sausage shapes in place for his arms.

Make two tiny flattened white fondant disks for his eyes and one black disk for a nose and stick in position. Paint in the pupils with black food coloring. Stick a small ball of brown fondant on top of the head for an ear and add detail with the end of a paintbrush.

Roll ⅛ oz red ready-to-roll fondant into a sausage. Cut this in half to make Santa's arms and stick these in position on his body. Make two tiny flesh-colored oval shapes for his hands and stick these on the ends of the arms.

7   Make another five teddy bears in the same way (you will probably find it easier to make these away from the cake and to stick them in position when they are finished). On the three unfinished bears, omit the ears and give each a glum-looking

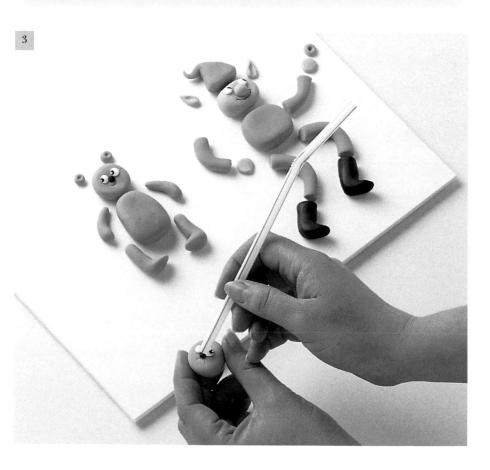

# 3

# Dozy Dad

*Unless they have a hobby, men can be difficult subjects to make cakes for. This is a neat solution, ideal for a birthday or Father's Day. If it's children that harangue him rather than a cat, substitute a child climbing over the back instead.*

## ■ INGREDIENTS

- Confectioner's sugar for rolling out
- 5½ oz white ready-to-roll fondant (see page 98)
- 6-in round sponge cake (see pages 94-97)
- ½ quantity butter cream (see page 98)
- 12½ oz pale blue ready-to-roll fondant
- 2¾ oz gray ready-to-roll fondant
- ¾ oz black ready-to-roll fondant
- 2¾ oz green ready-to-roll fondant
- 1 oz flesh-colored ready-to-roll fondant
- Black food coloring
- 1¼ oz brown ready-to-roll fondant

## ■ UTENSILS

- 8-in round cake board
- Water and paintbrush
- Rolling pin
- Small sharp knife
- Carving knife
- Spatula or cake server (optional)
- Cake spatula
- Toothpick (optional)
- Drinking straw

1 Cover the board with white ready-to-roll fondant as on page 100. Trim off excess and put the board to one side (*fig 1*).

2 Cut the cake into shape by slicing off about one third. Place the smaller, cutaway piece flat side down on the remaining section of cake to form the basic seat shape (*fig 2*). If there is not much seat area, slice a thin section away from the back of the chair. "Glue" the two sections of seat together with butter cream. Spread a layer of butter cream over the outside of the cake.

3 Knead and roll out 10½ oz pale blue ready-to-roll fondant. Carefully lift up the fondant and place over the cake. To prevent air being trapped, start from the central seat area and smooth the fondant into position. You may find that fondant gathers into folds at the back of the chair. These can usually be eased out by gently lifting and fanning the fondant out slightly. Trim and neaten the base.

4 Carefully lift and place the cake towards the back of the covered cake board. If you're worried about getting fingerprints in the fondant, use a spatula to lift it.

5 Roll out about 2 oz of the pale blue ready-to-roll fondant. Cut out a strip about 18 in x 1¼ in. Ideally the strip should be slightly wavy down one of the longest sides. This is not essential but it does make for a better frill. Making sure you have plenty of confectioner's sugar on the work surface to prevent the frill from sticking, roll a paintbrush or toothpick backwards and forwards over the wavy edge of the strip (*fig 3*). Paint a line of water around the side of the cake, about ¼ in up from the base. Stick the frill around the cake. Neaten the join by pushing the end of a paintbrush along the top of the strip to leave a circular pattern.

6 To make the cushions, roll out about 2 oz white ready-to-roll fondant fairly thickly. Cut out three squares about 2½ in square. Tweak the ends slightly and using the end of a drinking straw, poke four small circles into each one to look like buttons (*fig 4*). Stick the cushions onto the back of the chair.

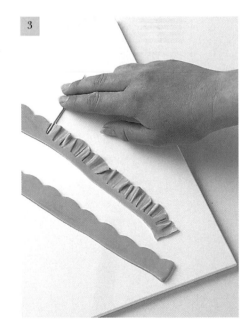

7 To make the man himself, begin with his legs. Roll 2¾ oz gray ready-to-roll fondant into a long sausage. Cut the sausage in half and stick it onto the chair. Roll two ¼ oz lumps of black fondant into oval shapes for his feet and stick one on the end of each leg.

# Decorating variation

A sofa chair is not just for people to snooze in — in fact, once you have made the basic shape you could set virtually anything on it. The cat in this variation looks especially at home! Make a potato like those in the flowerpot cake (page 68), decorate it with eyes and a mouth, sit it on the seat and you have an amusing couch-potato cake. A chair cake is an extremely useful shape to add to your repertoire because it provides an easy way to put full-length, upright figures onto a cake without having to fiddle about with awkward supports inside them.

10 To make the newspaper, cut a flat rectangle out of ¼ oz white fondant. Fold the fondant in half, then half again. Paint squiggles onto the newspaper with black food coloring to resemble the print and stick the paper onto the man's lap.

11 To make the cat, roll about ⅛ oz brown ready-to-roll fondant into a tapering sausage shape for his body. Pinch a couple of small ears out of the thicker end.

Stick two tiny strings of brown fondant onto the back of the chair for his paws and stick the body on top. Roll another tiny piece of fondant into a string for his tail. Paint on the cat's features and stripes neatly with some black food coloring.

**4**

as I did, that the head flops backwards, simply prop it up with a small triangle of white fondant which will just look like another cushion. Push the end of a paintbrush into the lower part of the head and pull it down slightly to give him an open-mouthed expression.

Stick a small ball of fondant on the front of the face for his nose and two at the sides for his ears. Add a little detail to the ears by making a small hollow with the end of a paintbrush. Either paint in the eyes with black food coloring or press two semi-circular impressions into the face using the drinking straw held at an angle.

Add two flattened balls of flesh-colored fondant for his hands.

**6**

8 Make his body by rolling 2 oz green ready-to-roll fondant into a conical shape and stick this on top of the legs (*fig 5*). Roll out a thin strip of the same color green and press vertical lines into the strip using the back of your knife. Lay this around the base of his jumper. Make a polo neck by sticking a small but thick disk of green fondant on top of the jumper and again press a few vertical lines around the edge.

For his arms, roll ¾ oz of the green fondant into a sausage. Cut it in half and arrange and stick the arms in whatever position you wish.

9 To make the man's head, roll ¾ oz flesh-colored ready-to-roll fondant into a ball (*fig 6*). Stick this onto the neck. If you find,

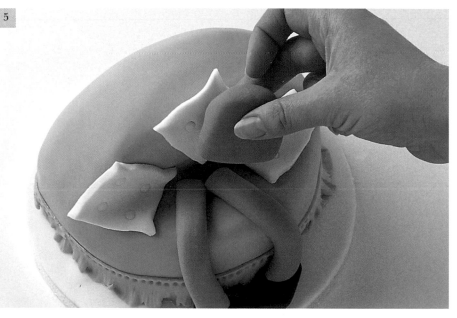

**5**

# Piggy bank

*Here's a cake to appeal to anyone with an interest in money, from the youngest saver to the most hard-bitten of accountants. To make the pig more dramatic, paint a pattern on his back using food colors or stick on fondant shapes.*

## INGREDIENTS

- Confectioner's sugar for rolling out
- 7 oz green ready-to-roll fondant
- Cake baked in a pudding bowl (see page 94)
- ½ quantity butter cream (see page 98)
- 12 oz pink ready-to-roll fondant
- ¼ oz white ready-to-roll fondant
- ¾ oz black ready-to-roll fondant
- About 7 oz, or 4 small bags, of chocolate coins
- 1 tbsp classic fondant icing (optional)

## UTENSILS

- 10-in round cake board
- Water and paintbrush
- Rolling pin
- Small sharp knife
- Piping nozzle
- Drinking straw
- Wooden spoon
- Large circle cutter (optional)
- Ear templates, if necessary (see page 109)

1 Cover the cake board with green ready-to-roll fondant as explained on page 100. Trim and neaten the edges, then place the covered board to one side.

2 Slice and fill the center of the cake with butter cream. Reassemble the cake and spread a layer of butter cream over the top and sides. Roll out and cover the cake with 8¾ oz pink ready-to-roll fondant. Trim and neaten the base, then place the cake towards the rear of the covered cake board.

3 Make a simple floral pattern on the pig's back by pressing something circular (such as an piping nozzle or small circle cutter) into the fondant while it is still pliable, then surrounding it with smaller circles made from a drinking straw (fig 1).

4 To make his face (fig 2), thinly roll out ¼ oz white ready-to-roll fondant. Cut out two disks about 1 in in diameter. Stick these to the front of the pig. Roll out the black fondant and cut out two smaller disks and a small rectangle for the money slot. Stick the circles onto his eyes and the slot in the middle of his back. Finish off each eye with a tiny flattened ball of white fondant as a highlight.

5 For his snout, roll and shape 1¾ oz pink ready-to-roll fondant into a thick disk about 2½ inches in diameter. Stick this to the front of his face. Don't use too much water

to do this or the snout will start to slide. Using the end of a wooden spoon, press two nostrils into the snout. Make a mouth either by pressing something circular into the fondant (such as a cutter) or by using the back of a knife to make a curved line. Make two small cuts at each end of the mouth.

6 Make a tail by rolling about ⅛ oz pink fondant into a tapering sausage shape. Bend it into a curly tail shape and stick to the back of the pig.

7 To make the pig's ears, roll out 1¾ oz pink ready-to-roll fondant to a thickness of about ¼ in. Cut out an ear shape, using the template if necessary. Scrunch up the leftover fondant and cut out a second ear. Stick the ears to the sides of the head, allowing them to fold over slightly at the top (fig 3).

8 Cut one of the chocolate coins in half and press it into the money slot. A drop of water should be enough to hold it in place but you could use a dab of classic fondant icing if you prefer. Arrange the rest of the coins around the board.

## TIP

*If you don't have any classic fondant icing readily available for sticking on the coins, use leftover butter cream instead — it will hold them in place just as well.*

# Baby cake

*If you're worried about piping directly onto the top of this cake, two methods of writing in icing are also shown. Read the instructions in step 1 first and see which one suits you best.*

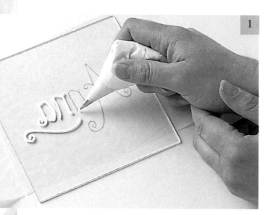

1   If you feel confident enough to pipe the baby's name directly onto the top of the cake without following a guide, go straight to step 2. If you're not, then one of these two solutions might help.

(a) Do this after you have covered the cake with ready-to-roll fondant. Write the baby's name on a piece of waxed paper. Place the paper, right side up, on the top of the cake and using either a toothpick, dressmaking pin or scriber (this is a sugarcraft tool especially designed for the job), trace over the lettering. Lift off the waxed paper and a scratched impression of the name should be left behind on the fondant.

Place about 1 tbsp classic fondant icing into a piping bag fitted with a number 2 piping nozzle and secure the end. Pipe over the lettering.

This method works best on a cake covered in rolled fondant that has been allowed to harden overnight. Otherwise it is very easy to dent the cake accidentally when leaning on it.

(b) Prepare this before you cover the cake with the fondant.

Write the baby's name on waxed paper. Turn the paper over so that the writing is still visible but now reads back to front. Place a small piece of plexiglass over the

waxed paper. Pipe over the name with classic fondant icing onto the plexiglass *(fig 1)*.

Put to one side, leave to dry and go on to step 2.

2   Level the top of the cake. Turn it upside down and place on the cake board. Slice and fill the center with butter cream. Reassemble the cake and butter cream the sides and top.

Dust the work surface with a little confectioner's sugar and knead and roll out 1 lb 2 oz yellow ready-to-roll fondant. Place this over the cake and carefully smooth it into position. Run over the surface with a cake smoother, if you have one, to iron out any bumps. Alternatively, use the flat of your hand. Trim away any excess fondant from the base.

Lightly moisten the exposed cake board with a little water. Roll out 7 oz yellow fondant and cut out a strip approximately 24 in long and 1¼ in wide. Carefully roll up the fondant strip, then unwind it to cover the cake board (see page 100). If you find this too time-consuming, you can leave the base uncovered.

## ■ INGREDIENTS

- Classic fondant icing (see page 99)
- 10-in round sponge cake (see pages 94-97)
- 1 quantity butter cream (see page 98)
- Confectioner's sugar for rolling out
- 1 lb 9 oz yellow ready-to-roll fondant (see page 98)
- 3½ oz flesh-colored ready-to-roll fondant
- 2 oz light brown ready-to-roll fondant
- 2 oz darker brown ready-to-roll fondant
- 1¼ oz pale blue ready-to-roll fondant
- ½ oz white ready-to-roll fondant
- Black food coloring
- 20 small candies

## ■ UTENSILS

- Waxed paper
- Pencil
- Eraser
- Sheet of clear plexiglass (about 8 in x 5 in) (optional)
- Pin or scriber (optional)
- Piping bags (see page 102 for details)
- Scissors
- Number 2 or 3 piping nozzles
- Clean damp cloth
- Carving knife
- 10-in round cake board
- Rolling pin
- Cake smoother (optional)
- Small sharp knife
- Water
- Medium and fine paintbrushes
- Toothpick
- 60 in white ribbon

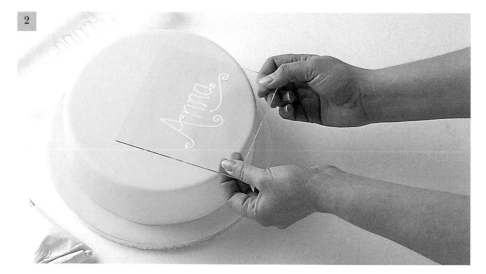

board. Starting from the back of the cake, hold the piping bag at a slight angle. Squeeze out a little classic fondant icing, then release the pressure and pull slightly. Keep the tip of the nozzle in the icing all the time. Squeeze out a little more icing, release the pressure and pull (*fig 3*). Repeat all the way around the base of the cake.

You may wish to practice this technique on your work surface first if you are not too confident of your piping skills. Alternatively, pipe a simple line of dots or stick candies on the cake instead.

5 All the babies, dressed or undressed, are composed of the same six basic shapes (*fig 4*). To make the babies' body, roll ¾ oz flesh-colored ready-to-roll fondant into a conical shape. Make the head by rolling ⅛ oz of flesh-colored fondant into a small ball. Stick in place with a little water (*fig 5*).

Make the babies' legs by rolling approximately ¼ oz flesh-colored fondant into a sausage. Cut this in two,

3 If using the second method of writing, gently touch the classic fondant icing on the plexiglass to check that it has dried. If it still feels soft, then place a bit of plastic wrap over the top of the cake to stop the rolled fondant surface from hardening too much before the piping is ready. (The rolled fondant has to be soft enough to take an impression.) When the piping feels hard to the touch, turn the plexiglass over and press the lettering into the top of the cake (*fig 2*). Carefully pull it away. The baby's name should now be visible as an impression. Pipe over the name with white classic fondant icing, using a number 2 nozzle.

4 When the name is on the top of the cake, pipe a "snail trail" around the base of the cake to hide the join between cake and

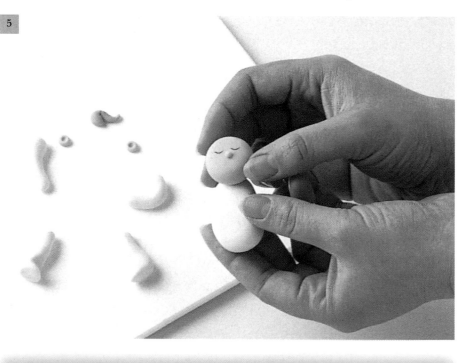

> **TIP**
> *To avoid damaging the rolled fondant cake, you may find it easier to make the models of the babies away from the cake and then stick them in position once they are finished.*

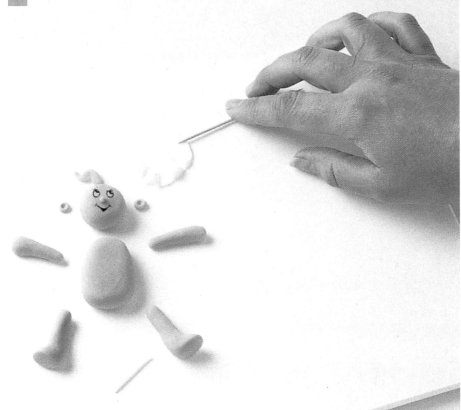

then gently bend the end of each one to form a foot. Stick these in whatever position you wish.

For the arms, take about ⅛ oz ready-to-roll fondant and roll into a sausage. Cut in two and flatten one end of each half to make a hand. Stick these against the body. Thinly roll out a little white fondant and cut out a tiny triangle. Stick this on as a diaper.

Paint the facial details with black food coloring and a fine paintbrush, and stick two tiny dots of fondant either side of the head for the ears and one in the middle of the face for a nose. To make a frilly mop hat, simply cut out a thin disk of white fondant and roll a toothpick around the edge to frill it (*fig 6*). Stick onto the back of the head and roll a tiny bit of yellow fondant into a curl and stick onto the forehead.

6   Make as many or as few babies as you want (or you have time for), altering the positions of the hands and feet and giving each one an individual expression and different hair color.

Use the same shapes for the baby in the romper suit, but use colored fondant for the arms, legs and body to look like the clothing.

7   To complete the cake, stick small candies around the top and the board, and tie a bow around the sides as the perfect finishing touch.

# Decorating variation

As you can see, this cake works just as well in a different color. If you prefer something paler, leave the base of the cake white and color the piping instead. If you find it difficult to tie a bow, leave it off and add a couple more babies and candies to fill the space instead.

# Twitcher

*There's a type of person who at the mere rumor of a lesser-spotted swamp gurgler near Natagocher will miss appointments, cross continents and sit for hours in freezing conditions just to catch the merest sight. Weird, but it makes for a good cake!*

1

## ■ INGREDIENTS

- 1 pudding bowl cake (see page 94)
- 1 quantity butter cream (see page 98)
- Confectioner's sugar for rolling out
- 9 oz black ready-to-roll fondant (see page 98)
- ¾ oz pale blue ready-to-roll fondant
- ¼ oz flesh-colored ready-to-roll fondant
- 2 oz brown ready-to-roll fondant
- ¼ oz white ready-to-roll fondant
- Black food coloring
- 5 oz dark green ready-to-roll fondant
- 5 oz mid-green ready-to-roll fondant
- 5 oz pale green ready-to-roll fondant
- Brown food coloring
- ¼ oz pale brown ready-to-roll fondant
- ¼ oz very dark brown ready-to-roll fondant
- ¾ oz yellow ready-to-roll fondant
- 1 oz golden brown ready-to-roll fondant
- 1 oz green-colored shredded coconut (see page 98)
- 1 oz brown-colored shredded coconut (see page 98)

## ■ UTENSILS

- Carving knife
- 10-in round cake board
- Cake spatula
- Rolling pin
- Water
- Medium and fine paintbrushes
- Small sharp knife
- Piping nozzle

1  Turn the cake upside down so that the widest part sits on the board. If it wobbles, cut a slice from the base so that it sits securely. Split it in half and fill the center with butter cream and reassemble. Position the cake to the left of the board and then spread a layer of butter cream over the sides and top.

2  Dust the work surface with confectioner's sugar. Knead 9 oz black ready-to-roll fondant until it is pliable. Roll it out and place over the cake. Smooth it into position, and trim and neaten the base.

3  To make the twitcher, begin with his binoculars. Roll ⅛ oz black ready-to-roll fondant into a small sausage. Cut this in half and stick the two halves side by side, pointing outwards, on the front of the cake. If they start to droop at all, stick a little ledge of black fondant underneath them to provide extra support.

Next, roll ¾ oz pale blue fondant into a sausage. Cut this in half and bend each half slightly into a curved boom-erang shape. Stick these pieces onto the cake with the flat, cut ends up against the binoculars.

4  To make the twitcher's head, roll a ⅛ oz lump of flesh-colored ready-to-roll fondant into a semi-circular shape. Stick this just above the binoculars.

Next, make two tiny flattened ovals of flesh-colored fondant for his hands and stick these on top of the binoculars. Thinly roll out a little brown fondant. Cut out and fringe a tiny rectangle. Stick this on top of his head *(fig 2)*.

To make his ears, stick two tiny balls of flesh-colored fondant either side of his head and push the end of a paintbrush into each ear to add detail.

Thinly roll out a little white fondant and cut out two tiny disks (a piping nozzle is useful for doing this). Stick the white circles to the ends of the binoculars and paint a small picture of a bird with black food coloring (you can leave this stage out if you wish).

5  Roll out a small piece of each of the green ready-to-roll fondants and cut out some

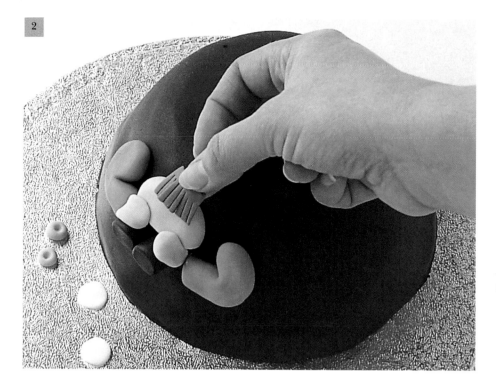

Cut out a diamond shape for his beak. Bend it in half and stick onto the face. Stick two tiny flattened balls of white fondant onto his face for his eyes and paint in pupils and eyebrows with black food coloring.

Roll out and cut two longish triangles for his wings and stick these either side of his body in an outraged, hands-on-hips position. Carefully place the bird on top of the cake.

9  Moisten the cake board with a little water and carefully spoon the colored coconut around the base of the cake to look like grass and earth.

**TIP**

*If the person you are making this cake for "twitches" for something else, substitute flowers or butterflies or a train for the bird.*

basic leaf shapes. Press a simple vein pattern into each one using the back of a knife. Starting from the base, stick the leaves around the sides of the cake, alternating the different shades and allowing them to overlap until the entire cake has been covered (*fig 2*).

6  To make the tree stump, mold 1¾ oz brown ready-to-roll fondant into a rounded stump shape with a flat base and top (*fig 1*). Holding the back of a knife vertically, press irregular lines around the sides of the stump. Paint a wash of watered-down brown food coloring around the stump to pick out the bark.

Cut out a thin disk of pale brown fondant and stick on top of the stump. Paint a few age rings on the top with brown food coloring.

Roll some little bits of leftover green fondant into thin strings and stick these up against the sides of the stump. Place it in position on the board and secure with a little water.

7  To make the smaller bird, roll about ⅛ oz very dark brown fondant into a tapering sausage shape (*fig 1*). Bend the head end up slightly and flatten and pull the tail into a point.

Add two tiny flattened balls of white fondant for his eyes and a tiny triangle of yellow for a beak. Stick two tiny dark brown triangles either side of the body for wings. Paint the pupils on the eyes with black food coloring.

8  For the large bird, use 1 oz golden-brown fondant. Mold this into a rounded cone. Bend the smaller end over to make a head (*fig 1*).

Roll out a little yellow fondant and cut out a rectangle for the tail. Cut a triangle out of one end and stick it against the back of the bird.

# Bride and groom

*A special feature of this cake is that as the models are on a thin cake board, they can be lifted off and kept as mementoes. If you prefer a rich fruit cake instead of sponge, cover with a layer of almond paste first.*

### ■ INGREDIENTS

- 8-in round sponge cake (see page 98)
- 1 quantity butter cream (see page 98)
- Confectioner's sugar for rolling out
- 1 lb 12 oz cream-colored ready-to-roll fondant
- 3 oz gray ready-to-roll fondant
- 2 strands raw dried spaghetti
- 1 oz flesh-colored ready-to-roll fondant
- 5 oz white ready-to-roll fondant
- ¼ oz pink ready-to-roll fondant
- ⅛ oz brown ready-to-roll fondant
- Black and gooseberry green food color pastes
- 1 oz black ready-to-roll fondant
- ⅛ oz yellow ready-to-roll fondant
- 3 oz green ready-to-roll fondant
- ½ quantity classic fondant icing (see page 99)

### ■ UTENSILS

- Carving knife
- 10-in round cake board
- Rolling pin
- Cake smoother (optional)
- Small sharp knife
- 6-in round thin cake board
- Water
- Fine and medium paintbrushes
- Templates for shirt, jacket and veil (see page 109)
- 2 piping bags (see page 102)
- 60 in ivory ribbon

1  Level the top of the cake, spread with butter cream and cover both the cake and board with 1 lb 9 oz cream-colored ready-to-roll fondant as described in step 2 of the baby cake on page 50. Place the cake to one side.

2  Cover the thin 6-in round cake board with 2 oz cream-colored fondant as described on page 100. Trim and neaten the edges. Place this to one side too.

3  On a spare board or work surface, make the groom. Roll 2¾ oz gray fondant into a chunky conical shape about 2¼ in tall. Check that the base is flat so that it stands upright. To add extra internal support, insert a strand of dried spaghetti into the body, leaving about 1½ in protruding out of the top (*fig 1*).

4  Roll ½ oz flesh-colored fondant into an oval (*fig 2*). Stick onto the body (use a little water as well), leaving about ⅜ in of spaghetti still protruding.
   Make his shirt by rolling out about ¼ oz of white fondant and cutting out a rectangle, using the template if necessary. Make a little cut in the center of the top edge. Stick this to the front of the body, allowing the collar

to just overlap the face. Bend the collar forwards slightly.

5  To make the cravat, roll a tiny piece of pink fondant into a thin string. Stick this just under the collar. Roll out a little more pink and cut into a thin, tapering rectangular shape. Press lines down the length of the strip using the back of a knife. Stick this in place on the front of the shirt (*fig 3*).

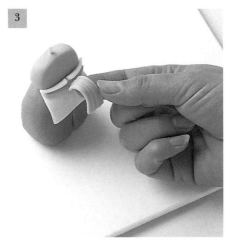

6  Roll out a tiny strip of brown fondant. Cut out a thinnish rectangle and press lines down its length. Moisten the top of the head and lay this across for his hair.

Stick three tiny balls of flesh-colored fondant on the head for his ears and nose and push the end of a paintbrush into each ear to add detail. Paint his features with black food coloring.
   To make the hat, roll out ¼ oz gray fondant. Cut out a circle about 1½ in in diameter and stick onto the head. Re-knead the rest of the gray and mold into a rounded shape with a flat base and top. Stick onto the head and bend up the sides of the brim.

7  To make the jacket, roll out ¾ oz of the black fondant. Cut out a jacket shape, using the template if necessary. Make a cut for the tails and wrap and stick the jacket around the groom's body (any gaps in the tummy area will be hidden by his arm at a later stage). Place the groom to one side.

front to make a bouquet. Intersperse the flowers with tiny bits of green fondant. Push little hollows in each flower with the end of a paintbrush.

11 Stick the bride and groom next to each other on the covered board and then make the groom's arms. Roll ¼ oz black fondant into a sausage. Cut it in two. Bend one half into a right-angle and stick on the front of the groom. Position and stick the other one so that it looks as though the groom has his arm around the bride (fig 6).

   Add two flattened balls of flesh-colored fondant for the hands.

8 Make the bride's skirt by rolling 2 oz white ready-to-roll fondant into a pointed conical shape. Stick a ⅛-oz oval of white fondant on top (fig 1). Insert a strand of dried spaghetti as you did for the groom. Roll ⅛ oz flesh-colored fondant into a ball for her head (fig 4) and stick it to the body. Paint her features with black food coloring and a fine brush and stick a tiny piece of flesh-colored fondant on the front of her face for a nose. Roll a little flesh-colored fondant into a thin sausage for her arms. Stick this onto the front of the body in a "U" shape.

9 To make the hair, roll a little yellow fondant into a thin strip about 2½ in long.

12 To make a rose, use about ¼ oz white or cream fondant. Roll the fondant into a thin strip. Paint a line of water down one side and roll up the fondant (fig 7). Tweak the petals into position and slice a little away from the base so the rose can stand up. Make a total of at least eight roses in this way.

Press lines into it with a knife, then lay and stick it over the bride's head (fig 5). Tweak the ends up into a curl. Make a tiny yellow rectangle for bangs. Press lines into this also and stick on her forehead.

10 To make her veil, roll out ½ oz white fondant. Cut out a veil, using the template if necessary. Moisten the bride's head and back and stick it in place.

   Stick a line of tiny pink rolled fondant balls along the edge of the veil and one on the groom's jacket as a button-hole. Also stick some on the bride's

13 To make a bud, roll about ⅛ oz of fondant into a sausage with two pointed ends. Press a line down the top and bend it into an "S" shape.

14 For the leaves, roll out a little of the green fondant and cut out a few very basic leaf shapes. Press a simple vein pattern into each one with the back of a knife, and stick the roses, leaves and buds around the bride and groom. Add little swirls of green food coloring and dots of classic fondant icing, too, if you like.

# Little monster

*Not only is this a quick cake to make but it's a useful one because you can use odd bits of colored rolled fondant to cover the monster. This cake was designed as a child's cake, but I know quite a few grown-up monsters it would suit too!*

## INGREDIENTS

- 1 pudding bowl cake (see page 94)
- 1 quantity butter cream (see page 98)
- Confectioner's sugar for rolling out
- 14 oz multi-colored mixture of various colored ready-to-roll fondants (e.g., green, white, orange, blue, yellow and red) (see page 98)
- 4 oz white ready-to-roll fondant
- 1 oz black ready-to-roll fondant
- Red food coloring
- Licorice or strawberry shoelace
- 3½ oz colored sugar or multi-colored candy balls

## UTENSILS

- Carving knife
- 10-in round cake board
- Rolling pin
- Small sharp knife
- Piping nozzle
- Water
- Medium and fine paintbrushes
- Toothpick

1 Place the cake upside down with the widest part forming the base and cut irregular lumps and bumps out of the cake (*fig 1*). Slice and fill the middle of the cake with a layer of butter cream. Reassemble the cake and place it on the board. "Glue" the cut-out lumps around the sides and top of the cake with butter cream. Spread a layer of butter cream over the top and sides.

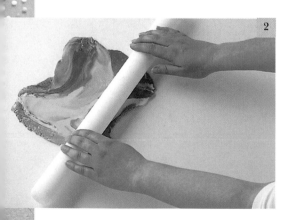

2 Roll out 10½ oz of the multi-colored fondant (*fig 2*) and use this to cover the cake. Smooth it into position over the cake, taking care to press out any air trapped in the hollows. Trim, neaten, and cut the excess from the base. Add the effect of scales by pressing something circular, such as a cutter or a piping nozzle held at an angle, into the fondant.

3 To make his eyes, take two ¾-oz lumps of white fondant. Roll them both into ball shapes, then flatten slightly. Stick them on the front of his face.

Roll out ¼ oz black ready-to-roll fondant and cut out two flat disks (your piping nozzle will come in useful again to do this). Stick the disks onto the eyes. Flatten two tiny balls of white fondant and stick these onto the black for highlights. Finish off each eye by painting a few ghoulish blood vessels with red food coloring and a fine paintbrush (*fig 3*).

4 To make his whiskers, cut licorice or strawberry shoelace into twelve shortish sections of between 2 in and 3½ in. Poke three holes above and below each eye using a toothpick, and insert a length of shoelace into each one.

5 For his ears, take 4 oz of the multi-colored ready-to-roll fondant. Divide it in two and mold each half into a slightly misshapen triangular shape. Stick the ears to the sides of the head.

6 Roll ¼ oz of the multi-colored ready-to-roll fondant into a round ball and stick onto the front of the face to make the monster's nose.

7 To make the mouth, thinly roll out ¾ oz black ready-to-roll fondant and cut out a devilish smiling shape. Stick this onto the face. Roll out ¼ oz white fondant and cut out three rectangles of slightly different sizes. Stick these onto the mouth to give the monster a gap-toothed smile.

8 To make the hands, roll ¾ oz white ready-to-roll fondant into a ball, then flatten it slightly. Cut the resulting disk in half. Make three partial cuts into each semi-circle and then splay the cuts out to make the fingers. Stick one hand on either side of the body.

9 To make the feet, take ¾ oz white ready-to-roll fondant. Roll it into a flattish circle the same as for the hands and cut it in half. Stick the two semi-circles against the monster's body. Press some lines into each foot using the back of a knife.

10 Lightly moisten the exposed cake board with a little water and sprinkle with colored sugar or multi-colored candy balls.

# Sports car

*This will suit anyone with a passion for fast cars and will disappear off the tea table speedily too! It's also very versatile — see how the basic shape can be adapted into an airplane (page 65). The rocks double up as candle holders.*

### ■ INGREDIENTS

- Cake baked in loaf pan (see page 94 for details)
- 1 quantity butter cream (see page 98)
- Confectioner's sugar for rolling out
- 9 oz green ready-to-roll fondant (see page 98)
- 4½ oz flesh-colored ready-to-roll fondant
- 3¾ oz brown ready-to-roll fondant
- 4 oz white ready-to-roll fondant
- 5 oz black ready-to-roll fondant
- 1½ oz gray ready-to-roll fondant
- 1½ oz cream ready-to-roll fondant
- Black and green food color pastes
- 2 oz shredded coconut

### ■ UTENSILS

- Carving knife
- Cake spatula
- 10-in square cake board
- Rolling pin
- Small sharp knife
- Water and paintbrush
- Circle cutters or similar
- 2 small bowls

1 Stand the cake up with the thinnest part at the bottom. Cut two triangular pieces away from the sides to form the hood. Cut a slope into the top of the hood too. Level the remaining top section of the cake where the driver will eventually sit and round all the top edges slightly to form the basic shape *(fig 1)*.

Slice and fill the middle of the cake with butter cream. Reassemble and place it diagonally on the cake board. Spread a thin layer of butter cream over the top and sides of the cake.

2 Dust the work surface with confectioner's sugar and knead and roll out the green ready-to-roll fondant. Carefully lift this over the cake and gently smooth into position. Trim and neaten the base.

3 To make the driver, first roll 3½ oz flesh-colored ready-to-roll fondant into a flattish oval shape *(fig 2)*. Stick this with a little water towards the back of the car.

Roll 2½ oz brown fondant into a ball, then flatten the base to make a semi-circular shape for the driver's helmet. Stick this on top of his head. Roll out about another ¼ oz brown fondant and cut out a thin, flat semi-circle. Stick this to the front of the helmet to form the brim *(fig 3)*.

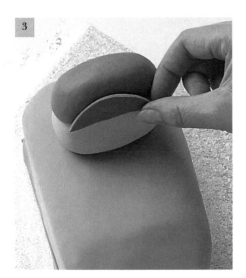

4 For the eyes, roll out ¼ oz white ready-to-roll fondant to a thickness of ¼ in and cut out two disks about ¾ in in diameter. If you don't have a circle cutter this size and can't find a lid or anything else to use as a cutter, simply divide the fondant into two, roll each half into a ball, then squash each ball down to the right size. Finish off the eyes by sticking two tiny flattened balls of black fondant onto the

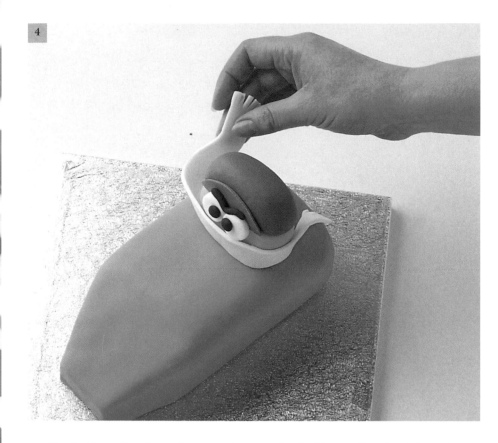

white for his pupils and a small sausage of black over the top for his eyebrows.

5 To make the scarf, roll out the cream fondant. Cut into a strip about 11 in x 1 in. Cut a fringe into both ends and paint a line of water around the driver's neck. Lay the scarf into position (*fig 4*). Tweak the ends up slightly into a jaunty, "blowing in the wind" angle.

6 Roll a pea-sized ball of flesh-colored ready-to-roll fondant and stick onto the driver's

face for his nose. Knead and shape about ¼ oz gray fondant into a thickish semi-circle for the steering wheel. Stick this in front of the driver.

Roll ¾ oz black fondant into a sausage about 10 in long. Starting from the back, lay and stick this on top of the car, around the driver (*fig 5*).

7 To make the driver's arms, roll about ½ oz brown ready-to-roll fondant into a sausage about 4 in long. Cut it in half. Make two partial cuts in the center of each arm at the

elbow and bend each one into a right-angle. Stick an arm on each side of the body.

Finish off the arms by sticking on a pair of hands made from small flattened circles of flesh-colored fondant. Arrange the hands so that they hold on to the steering wheel.

8 To make the ear flaps for the helmet, roll out approximately ½ oz brown ready-to-roll fondant. Cut out two small oval shapes. If you find cutting out an oval using the tip of your knife too difficult, cut out a circle instead using a small lid or circle cutter, then gently pull it into shape. Another method is to cut out a rectangle, slice off the corners and gently smooth the edges into an oval.

When you have made your oval shapes, stick one either side of the helmet for the flaps (*fig 6*). Next, cut two tiny strips for his helmet straps and stick one on either flap.

**TIP**

*To personalize your car, write the recipient's name, age or a short message on the number plate using black food color and a paintbrush.*

9  To make the wheels, roll out about
4¼ oz black ready-to-roll fondant to a
thickness of about ¼ in. Cut out two disks
about 2¼ in in diameter. Scrunch up the
leftover fondant. Re-roll it and cut out
another two disks. Stick the wheels into
position (fig 7).

Roll out about ¼ oz of white ready-
to-roll fondant and cut out four smaller
and much thinner disks. If you haven't
got anything suitable to cut out a
circle with, simply divide the fondant
into four. Roll each quarter into a
ball and flatten to the required size.
These circles form the centers of the
wheels. Stick them neatly into position.

10 For the bumpers, roll 1 oz gray ready-
to-roll fondant out to a thickness of
about ¼ in. Cut out two strips. The
first should measure about 3 in long
by ¾ in wide. Stick this around the front
of the car. The back bumper should
measure about 6 in x ¾ in. Stick this into
place too.

11 To make the headlights, take another
¼ oz gray ready-to-roll fondant and roll
this into an egg shape. Cut it in half
and stick both halves to the front of
the hood. Thinly roll out about ¾ oz
white fondant and cut out two small
disks. Stick one disk onto the front of
each headlight.

Also cut out two small rectangles for
the number plates and stick them to the
front and back of the car.

12 Place ¾ oz of the shredded coconut in one
of the bowls and color it green by mixing
in a little green food color paste. Color the
rest gray in another bowl with a little black
food color paste.

## Decorating variation

To adapt the car into an airplane, the same basic body shape was
covered with gray rolled fondant. The wings and tail were made out of
gray-colored gelatin icing (see page 99) and allowed to harden overnight.
(Turn the components over after about 4-5 hours to allow the undersides
to dry out as well.) They were attached to the body of the airplane with
classic fondant icing and supported by balls of scrunched-up plastic wrap
placed underneath the wings while drying in position. Add a propeller to
the front of the plane. Decorate the nose of the plane and the wings
with circles of colored rolled fondant. The cake board was covered in
pale blue fondant and decorated with white cut-out clouds and birds
painted in black food coloring.

Lightly moisten the exposed cake board
with a few drops of water. Carefully spoon
the gray coconut immediately around the
car, then spoon the green over the edges.
To make things easier and quicker, you
could color all the coconut just one shade
if you prefer.

13 Finally, to make the rocks, partially knead
about 2¾ oz white ready-to-roll fondant and
about ¾ oz black fondant together for a
marbled effect. Pull off irregular-sized
lumps and stick these along the side of the
road. These rocks can also be used as
candle holders.

# Chocolate box

A wonderful cake suitable for all sorts of occasions
– birthdays, Valentine's day, Mother's day, anniversaries
or any chocoholic type of day (and you don't need much of an excuse
for those!).

■ **INGREDIENTS**

- 6-in round sponge cake (see pages 94-97)
- 1 quantity butter cream (see page 98)
- Confectioner's sugar for rolling out
- 3 oz black ready-to-roll fondant (see page 98)
- 10 oz pink ready-to-roll fondant
- 1-oz bag white chocolate buttons
- ½-lb box milk chocolates
- 7 oz white ready-to-roll fondant

■ **UTENSILS**

- Carving knife
- 9-in round cake board
- Rolling pin
- 6-in round thin cake board
- Small sharp knife
- Ruler
- Heart-shaped cutter
- Drinking straw
- Water and paintbrush
- 30 in ribbon

1 Level the cake, if necessary, then turn it upside down and place onto the cake board. Slice and fill the center with butter cream and spread a thin layer of butter cream around the top and sides.

2 Knead and roll out all the black ready-to-roll fondant on a work surface dusted with confectioner's sugar. Using the thin 6-in cake board as a template, cut out a black disk and lay this on top of the cake. Clean your hands, rolling pin, and work surface to avoid getting black sooty smudges everywhere.

3 Measure the height of the cake. Sprinkle the work surface with confectioner's sugar and roll out 7 oz of pink fondant so that you can cut out a strip about 18 in long and about ½ in wider than the depth of your cake (this cake measured about 3½ in). Roll the fondant up like a bandage, making sure it is not too tight or you will have problems unwinding it. Dust with more confectioner's sugar if it seems to be sticking and then unwind it around the side of the cake (fig 1).

If the fondant won't stick, it probably means the previous butter cream covering around the sides has dried out, so simply spread another thin layer to provide better adhesion. Neaten and trim away any excess from the base and the join.

4 Using a heart-shaped cutter and a drinking straw, press a pattern around the side of the box.

5 Carefully paint a light line of water around the inside edge of the black disk. Neatly press a line of white chocolate buttons vertically into the black fondant, allowing them to rest against the pink fondant (fig 2).

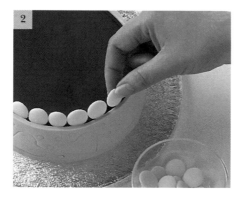

6 Arrange the chocolates in the top of the box, securing them in position with dabs of butter cream. Unfortunately, this arrangement uses up most of a ½-lb box of milk chocolates, leaving only a couple left over for the cook. Stick one of these on top of the chocolates to support the lid and sample the leftovers – all for purely professional taste-testing purposes, of course!

7 Moisten the top and sides of the thin cake board with a little water, roll out and cover with 3 oz of pink fondant. Trim and neaten the edges and press the heart cutter and

drinking straw into the fondant to echo the pattern around the sides. Place the lid to one side temporarily while you cover the base to avoid it from getting damaged.

8 Moisten the exposed cake board with a little water. Knead and roll 7 oz white fondant into a strip. Roll it up, then unwind it around the board allowing it to fall into folds like fabric as you go (see page 101). Press the fondant down neatly at the edges of the board and trim away any excess.

9 Place a small dab of butter cream on top of the highest chocolate. Place the lid in position on top.

10 Make a bow out of the ribbon and attach this to the cake with a little more butter cream.

> **TIP**
>
> *For a completely edible box (if you have time), you could make the lid out of pink-colored gelatin icing as shown on page 99 and decorate this with an icing bow.*

# Gardener's delight

A novel cake for budding gardeners. It could be decorated with flowers instead if you prefer — see page 57 for effective but extremely fast roses. If you're not keen on almond paste, this cake looks just as effective made up in rolled fondant.

### ■ INGREDIENTS

- Flowerpot-shaped cake (see step 1)
- 1 quantity butter cream (see page 98)
- Confectioner's sugar for rolling out
- 2 lb white almond paste
- Paprika, red, green, dark brown, black, orange and yellow food color pastes
- 2 oz dark brown sugar

### ■ UTENSILS

- 9-in round cake board
- Carving knife
- Cake spatula
- Rolling pin
- Tape measure
- Water and paintbrush
- Small sharp knife

1 The easiest way to make a cake of this shape is to bake the cake itself in a new 6-in terracotta plant pot. Simply wash the pot out, grease and line it with waxed paper. Use the same amounts given on page 94 for a 6-in-square cake. Level the top of the cake and turn upside down so the widest part sits on the cake board. Slice and fill the center with butter cream and spread extra butter cream around the top and sides.

2 Color 1 lb 4 oz almond paste terracotta using paprika food color paste. If you can't obtain paprika color, use a mixture of red, yellow and a hint of brown. Roll out 14 oz on a work surface dusted with confectioner's sugar and cover the cake. Smooth over the top and sides and trim any excess from the base.

3 Re-knead the excess into the rest of the terracotta-colored almond paste. Roll it out and cut out a strip about 18 in x 1½ in. Paint a line of water around the base of the cake. Wind up the almond paste strip like a bandage. Then, starting from the back, unwind it around the base of the cake so it resembles the lip of a real flowerpot (fig 1). Neaten the join.

4 To make the tomatoes, color 1¾ oz almond paste red. Roll into two balls and make a dent in the top of each one with the end of a paintbrush. Roll out about ⅛ oz green-colored almond paste and cut out two

rough star shapes. Stick one on the top of each tomato with a little water (fig 2).

5 For the potatoes, roll 4 oz white almond paste into two misshapen oval shapes. Leave them like this for the moment as they are easier to paint once in position.

6 For the carrots, color 2 oz almond paste orange. Divide into three and roll into carrot shapes. Press a few lines across the top using the back of a knife. Roll out ⅛ oz of green almond paste and cut out three irregular rectangles. Make cuts down almost the whole length of each shape and fringe. Stick one on each carrot.

7 For the peas, simply color about ¼ oz almond paste a pale green color and roll into small balls.

8 For the pepper, color 2¾ oz of almond paste yellow and roll into a conical shape. Press small grooves into the sides and top and finish with some green almond paste bent into a stalk.

9 Arrange the vegetables around the base of the flowerpot, securing them with a little

water. Make sure the join on the lip of the flowerpot is hidden at the back. Moisten the exposed cake board with a little water and spoon the dark brown sugar around the board to look like soil.

10 Paint the potatoes with a wash of watered-down brown food coloring. Finish with tiny dots of black food coloring and also paint a black circle on the top of the cake to look like the hole in the top of the flowerpot.

11 Roll out 1½ oz green almond paste and cut out some leaves. Press a few veins in each one using the back of a knife and stick these around the flowerpot.

# Funny bunnies

*On this design the cake and board are covered all in one go. If you don't feel comfortable doing it this way, cover the cake first and then the board separately. Hide any tears under rocks and rabbits later.*

## ■ INGREDIENTS

- 8-in round sponge cake (see pages 94-97)
- 1 quantity butter cream (see page 98)
- Confectioner's sugar for rolling out
- 1 lb 5 oz mid-green ready-to-roll fondant
- ¾ oz black ready-to-roll fondant
- 7 oz gray ready-to-roll fondant
- 2½ oz white ready-to-roll fondant
- ¼ oz flesh-colored ready-to-roll fondant
- 1¾ oz pink ready-to-roll fondant
- 1 oz orange ready-to-roll fondant
- ¼ oz dark green ready-to-roll fondant

## ■ UTENSILS

- Carving knife
- 10-in round cake board
- Cake spatula
- Water and paintbrush
- Rolling pin
- Small sharp knife
- Wooden spoon
- Five-petal flower cutter (optional)
- Piping nozzle

1 Carve the cake into an irregular shape by cutting out lumps and bumps *(fig 1)*. Place some of the cut-out pieces on top of the cake to increase its height and some around the edges. "Glue" all the cut-out pieces in place with dabs of butter cream, then slice and fill the middle of the cake with more butter cream. Spread a thin covering of butter cream over the outside of the cake as well.

2 Dust the work surface with confectioner's sugar and knead the mid-green ready-to-roll fondant until pliable. Lightly moisten the exposed cake board with a little water. Roll out the fondant, then lift and place it over both the cake and the board. Starting from the middle of the cake and trying to expel any trapped air, smooth the fondant into position. Trim and neaten the edges around the board.

3 To make the rabbit popping out of the burrow, first roll out about ¼ oz of the black fondant and cut out a flat disk about 2 in in diameter. Stick this on top of the cake with a little water.

Roll ⅛ oz gray fondant into a sausage, cut this in two and flatten both halves to make the paws. Stick these onto the edge of the burrow.

To make the head, roll 2 oz gray fondant into a cone. Flatten the cone slightly, making sure it can still stand upright. Make a cut from the tip of the cone to about one-third of the way down the center of the head. Pull the two sections apart slightly to make his ears and add detail by pressing a paintbrush lightly into each one *(fig 2)*. Stick the head onto the paws.

4 Roll out about ¼ oz white ready-to-roll fondant. Cut out a tiny rectangle for the rabbit's teeth and two small round disks for his eyes *(fig 2)* — a small piping nozzle is

Make arms for the sitting-up rabbit by rolling ⅛ oz gray fondant into a thin sausage. Cut it in half and stick the two paws as though they are holding the carrot. Roll out the dark green fondant and cut into small, thin strips. Fringe each strip and stick one on the end of each carrot.

8  To make the rocks, partially knead together ¾ oz gray fondant and 1¾ oz white fondant. Pull off small lumps and mold into irregular rock-like shapes. Dot these around the cake.

9  For the flowers, roll out a little pink fondant. If using the flower cutter, cut out a flower shape or if using a piping nozzle, cut out five pink circles and arrange them in a circle. Place the flower on the cake and top with a small central circle of white fondant. Make about six flowers in this way and position them around the cake.

useful for cutting out these. Make a small cut in the middle of the rectangle and stick both the teeth and the eyes in position. Make two tiny balls of black fondant and flatten them. Stick these onto the eyes for the pupils.

Roll out ⅛ oz flesh-colored ready-to-roll fondant and cut out two slightly larger circles for his muzzle. Stick these over the teeth. Finish off the rabbit's face with a tiny, flattened ball of pink fondant for a nose.

5  To make the seated rabbit, roll 2 oz gray ready-to-roll fondant into a flattish circle for the body. Stick this against the cake. Roll out about ⅛ oz white fondant and cut out a small circle. Stick this to his tummy.

Make another head as before and stick this onto the body. If the head starts to fall backwards, support it from behind with a bit of gray fondant, and tell anyone who spots it that it's a rock and is supposed to be there!

6  For his feet, roll two ¼ oz lumps of gray fondant into oval shapes, then flatten them both slightly. Stick them onto the front of the body and make three dents into the end of each one using the end of a wooden spoon or paintbrush. Cut out and stick a small white disk onto each foot too.

7  To make the carrots, divide the orange fondant into six and roll each bit into a carrot shape. Using the back of a knife, press a few lines into the top of each one (fig 3). Take a "bite" out of one using a piping nozzle. Stick the bitten carrot onto the front of the rabbit and the rest around the board.

### TIP

*This cake also introduces a five-petal flower cutter that, among other things, can be used to produce these marvelous bold cartoon-type flowers. These cutters are available from specialty cake shops but if you don't wish to buy one, an alternative method using a piping nozzle is also shown.*
*If you want to cut down on the modeling, have both bunnies popping out of burrows.*

# Horse and rider

*If making this cake for someone who owns a horse, try to copy the markings and hair color of the characters involved. To make a male rider, simply shorten the hair. You can substitute butter cream for the classic fondant icing if you wish.*

### ■ INGREDIENTS

- 6-in round sponge cake (see pages 94-97)
- ½ quantity butter cream (see page 98)
- Confectioner's sugar for rolling out
- 14 oz white ready-to-roll fondant (see page 98)
- 3½ oz golden-brown ready-to-roll fondant
- ¾ oz dark brown ready-to-roll fondant
- ¼ oz flesh-colored ready-to-roll fondant
- White classic fondant icing (optional) (see page 99)
- Black, blue, yellow (melon) and gooseberry-green food color pastes
- 1 oz black ready-to-roll fondant

### ■ UTENSILS

- Carving knife
- 8-in round cake board
- Cake spatula
- Rolling pin
- Small sharp knife
- Water and paintbrush
- 3 piping bags (see page 102)
- Scissors

1  Level the top of the cake and, if necessary, turn upside down and place in the middle of the cake board. Slice and fill the center of the cake with a layer of butter cream. Re-assemble the cake and then spread a thin covering of butter cream around the sides and top.

2  Dust the work surface with confectioner's sugar and knead and roll out 10½ oz white ready-to-roll fondant. Carefully lift the fondant and place it over the cake. Smooth it into position and trim and neaten the base. Place the cake to one side while you make the horse.

3  Begin with the body. Roll 2 oz golden-brown fondant into a tapering cone shape. Lay this on its side *(fig 1)*.

   Make the head out of ¾ oz golden-brown fondant. Pull off two tiny bits and keep for the ears. Roll the rest into an oval shape. Lightly squeeze the center to make one rounded end bigger than the other. This bigger end will form the horse's nose. Stick the head onto the body and make dents for nostrils using the end of a paintbrush.

4  Make a saddle out of ⅛ oz dark brown fondant. First cut out and stick a tiny, thin strip across the horse's back. Roll the rest of the dark brown fondant into an oval shape, then flatten it slightly. Stick this onto the horse's girth.

5  To make the forelegs, roll ¼ oz of the golden-brown fondant into a sausage. Cut this in two and bend each leg in half. Stick these against the body.

   To make the hind legs, roll ½ oz golden-brown fondant into a sausage approximately 4 in long. Again, divide the sausage in two and bend both halves. As you stick them against the sides of the horse, slightly flatten the top section of the leg.

Make two tiny triangular ears out of the leftover fondant and stick these onto the head. Press a paintbrush into each ear to add some detail. Carefully position the horse on top of the cake and secure in place with a little water.

6  To make the rider's head, take ¼ oz flesh-colored ready-to-roll fondant. Pull off a tiny piece for a nose and roll the rest into a ball. Stick the nose into position and paint eyes and a disgruntled mouth using black food coloring.

7  Partially mix a little blue food coloring into 2 tbsp of classic fondant icing and smear this on the top of the cake in a sort of

1

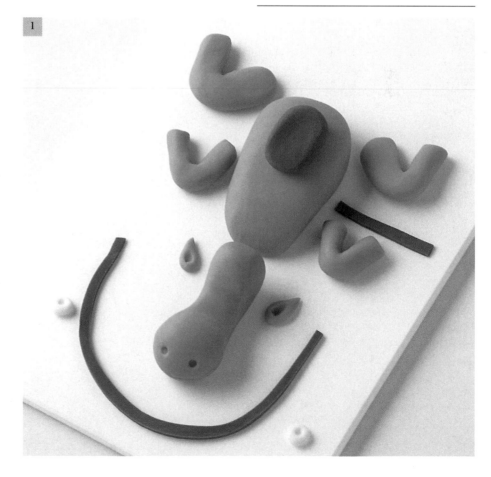

kidney shape. Place the rider's head in the water. Make her hair by rolling out a little dark brown fondant and cutting it into a rectangle. Press lines down the length of the rectangle with the back of a knife. Moisten the top of the rider's head and lay the hair in position (*fig 2*).

Make a riding hat by rolling ⅛ oz black fondant into a round lump, then flatten the base so that it will sit on her head. Pinch a peak into the front of the hat and stick in position.

8  Partially knead ¾ oz black ready-to-roll fondant into 3½ oz white fondant. Pull off little lumps and stick around the edge of the pond and the base of the cake to look like rocks.

Paint some watered-down green food coloring around the horse and pond (gooseberry food color paste is the ideal shade for this).

9  Mix a tiny bit of yellow food coloring into 1 tbsp of classic fondant icing to turn it

cream. Place the icing in a piping bag and snip about ⅛ in off the end. Pipe the horse's mane and tail using a squiggly motion (*fig 3*).

10 Color 2 tbsp classic fondant icing light green and place in a piping bag. Do the same with some darker green classic fondant icing. Snip the ends off both piping bags and pipe wiggly lines of greenery up the sides of the cake.

11 Finally, to finish off the horse, roll out a little dark brown ready-to-roll fondant. Cut out a long, thin strip for the horse's reins and lay this over the nose and around the back of the horse. Stick a tiny ball of white fondant either side of the mouth and push a small hole in each one using the end of a paintbrush.

### TIP

*If you have problems making piping bags, your local cake-decorating equipment shop should stock ready-made ones. Alternatively, you can buy tubes of "writing" icing which could also be used to make the mane and tail.*

# Golfing star

*A fun way of incorporating a person's favorite sport into a design is to base the cake itself on a piece of equipment such as a golf bag or a tennis racquet, then make a small model of the recipient dressed in the appropriate outfit.*

### ■ INGREDIENTS

- Confectioner's sugar for rolling out
- 10½ oz green ready-to-roll fondant
- 6-in square cake (see pages 94-97)
- 1 quantity butter cream (see page 98)
- 12½ oz white ready-to-roll fondant
- 2 oz gray ready-to-roll fondant
- 2¼ oz dark brown ready-to-roll fondant
- 3¼ oz red ready-to-roll fondant
- 2 oz light brown ready-to-roll fondant
- 1¾ oz blue ready-to-roll fondant
- 1 oz flesh-colored ready-to-roll fondant
- ¼ oz black ready-to-roll fondant

### ■ UTENSILS

- 12-in round cake board
- Water
- Paintbrush
- Rolling pin
- Small sharp knife
- Cake smoother (optional)
- Carving knife
- Cake server (optional)
- Cake spatula
- Piping nozzle

1  Moisten the cake board with a little water. Sprinkle some confectioner's sugar onto the work surface and knead the green ready-to-roll fondant until it becomes pliable. Begin to roll it out into a thick, flattish disc, then lift and place the fondant on the cake board. Continue to roll the fondant up to and over the edges of the board. Trim and neaten the edges.

If you possess one, run a cake smoother over the surface of the board to iron out any lumps and bumps. Alternatively, use the flat of your hand and strategically position the cake, figure, and golf clubs over the worst bits later! Place the covered board to one side.

2  Cut the cake into shape by slicing about 2 in off one side. Place this against one of the now shorter sides to increase the length of the bag. Now cut the cake into a more recognisable bag shape by making two diagonal cuts at the top of the bag to give it a tapering neck and also cut a slope into the neck of the bag (*fig 1*). Round all the corners slightly.

3  Slice and fill the middle of the cake with a layer of butter cream, then spread a thin covering of butter cream over the top and sides. Wipe away any crumbs from the work surface and dust with confectioner's sugar.

Knead and roll out 10½ oz white ready-to-roll fondant. Lift and place over the cake. Smooth the fondant into position and trim away any excess from the base. Carefully lift the cake and place on the covered cake board. (You may find using a cake server to lift the cake helps to prevent fingerprints on the fondant.)

4  Roll and shape about ¾ oz gray ready-to-roll fondant into a sort of tennis racquet shape. Bend the large, rounded end over to one side to make a golf club and stick onto the board at the neck of the bag.

To make the wooden club, roll 1½ oz brown fondant into a more rounded club shape. Stick a small flat oval of gray fondant onto the top of the club and stick into position. Press a few lines into the top of the first club using the back of a knife (*fig 2*).

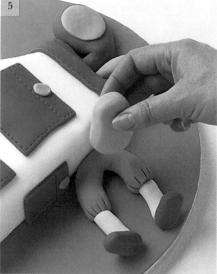

5  Roll out ¾ oz red ready-to-roll fondant and cut out a strip about 1 in x 5 in. Make a series of small cuts along the two longer sides using just the tip of your knife to look like stitching. Lightly moisten the back of the strip with a little water and lay this over the base of the golf clubs and the neck of the bag (*fig 3*).

6  Roll out a further 2½ oz red fondant and cut out three rectangles. The largest should be about 4 in x 3 in and the other two about 3 in x 2½ in. Stick these into position and press the back of a knife across each one to leave a line looking like a flap. Using the tip of your knife again, "stitch" around

each pocket (*fig 4*). Finish off each pocket with a button made from a small flattened ball of gray fondant.

7  To make the golfer himself, begin with his legs. Roll about 1½ oz light brown ready-to-roll fondant into a sausage about 5 in long. Slightly bend the sausage into a "U" shape and press a few lines into both ends to look like folds in the fabric. Stick this on the board towards the neck of the bag. Roll ¾ oz yellow fondant into a sausage and cut in half. Stick one onto the end of each leg for his socks. Roll two ¼ oz lumps of dark brown fondant into two oval shapes for his feet and stick one on the end of each sock.

Make a body by rolling about 1¾ oz of blue fondant into a cone and stick this on top of the legs (*fig 5*).

8  To make the arms, roll ¾ oz blue fondant into a sausage and cut in half. Stick one arm either side of the body, allowing them to rest on the legs and the side of the golf bag itself. Slightly flatten a small ball of blue fondant to make a thickish disc for the golfer's polo neck (*fig 6*). Stick this on top of the body.

9  Make a head by rolling ¼ oz flesh-colored ready-to-roll fondant into a ball. Stick this onto the neck. Give him a smiling mouth by pressing a piping nozzle or something similar into the lower part of the face and pulling it slightly downwards. His eyes are made by sticking two small discs of white fondant onto his face. Stick two smaller discs of blue onto the white and top with two even smaller discs of black fondant. Stick a tiny ball of flesh-

**TIP**
*Personalize the figure by coloring the hair and eyes the same color as the recipient's. Add any distinguishing features too, such as glasses, a beard or long hair.*

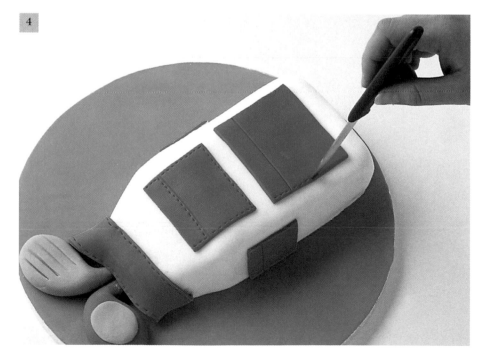

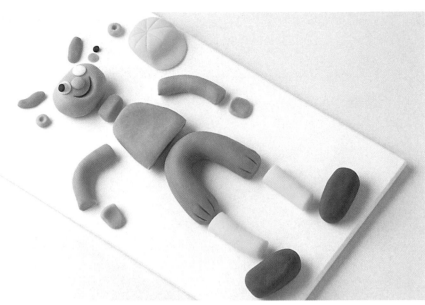

colored fondant onto the face for his nose and two on either side of the head for his ears. Press the end of a paintbrush into each ear to leave a small hollow. Stick a small oval of flesh-colored fondant onto the end of each arm for his hands.

10 Make hair by sticking a couple of tiny bits of light brown ready-to-roll fondant to the top of the head. To make the cap, roll ¼ oz of yellow fondant into a flattish oval shape. Tweak the front into a peak and press lines across the top in a sort of star shape. Top with a tiny ball of yellow fondant and stick on the top of the head. Decorate the front of the jumper and both socks with small, contrasting squares of blue and yellow ready-to-roll fondant.

11 To make the strap, thinly roll out 2 oz white ready-to-roll fondant and cut out a strip about 12 in x 1 in. "Stitch" along the edges of the strap in the same way as you did for the pockets, then lay the strap over the top of the bag *(fig 7)*. Use a little water to secure the handle in place.

12 Finally, finish the board with two tiny golf clubs made by rolling about ⅛ oz black fondant into a thin string for the handles. Cut this in half and stick onto the board. Make two tiny golf club heads out of a little brown and gray fondant.

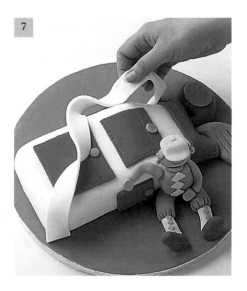

# Decorating variation

Another easy sports theme is a sports cap cake. The cake itself was baked in an ovenproof pudding bowl which automatically gave it an authentic rounded shape. It was covered with rolled fondant and a semi-circle of blue rolled fondant was placed on the board to look like its peak. It could be decorated with models from virtually any sport or you could paint a badge or emblem to stick on the front using food color.

# Teddy bear

It is possible to buy a ready-colored ready-to-roll fondant from cake-decorating shops that is aptly called "Teddy Bear Brown." If you can't get hold of this, use brown ready-to-roll fondant mixed with a little yellow and red for a similar color.

■ **INGREDIENTS**

- 6 in round sponge cake
- ½ quantity butter cream (see page 98)
- Confectioner's sugar for rolling out
- 2 lb golden-brown ready-to-roll fondant
- 2 candy sticks or strands of dried spaghetti
- ¼ oz white ready-to-roll fondant
- 1¾ oz black ready-to-roll fondant
- Black food coloring

■ **UTENSILS**

- Carving knife
- 8-in round cake board
- Rolling pin
- Small sharp knife
- Water and paintbrush
- Wooden spoon
- 39 in ribbon

Cut the cake to shape by lying it flat on its base and slicing off about a third of the cake. This section is then placed on top of the remaining cake so that it looks a bit like an "L" shape from the side.

2 Stick the two sections together with a little butter cream and, if you wish, slice the base cake through the middle and spread a layer of butter cream there as well. Then place the cake towards the rear of the cake board and spread a thin covering of butter cream over the entire cake.

3 Dust the work surface with confectioner's sugar and knead 10½ oz of the golden-brown fondant until pliable. Roll the fondant out, then lift and place it over the cake. Starting with the tummy area, to stop air bubbles getting trapped there, smooth the fondant into position over the cake. You may find that the fondant falls into folds at the back. By gently lifting and pulling it you should be able to smooth these out. Trim and neaten the base.

4 To provide support for the head, insert two candy sticks into the top of the body leaving about half the stick protruding (fig 1). If you can't get hold of candy sticks (or sweet cigarettes, as they used to be called), use some shortened strands of raw, dried spaghetti instead. Lightly moisten the area around the candy sticks with water to help keep the head in position, but don't use too much or the head will slide about.

5 Make the head by rolling 10½ oz ready-to-roll fondant into a ball. Flatten the ball to make a thick disk and slot the head into position onto the candy sticks.

6 Roll another 3 oz golden-brown fondant into an oval for the muzzle. Stick this to the lower part of the face.

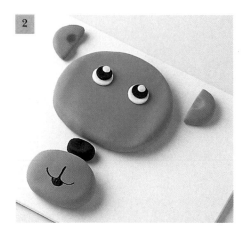

7 To make the ears, roll 1 oz golden-brown fondant into a ball. Flatten the ball into an oval and cut in half. To add detail, press a rounded hollow into each ear using a wooden spoon handle (fig 2) and stick one either side of the head with a little water.

8 To make the eyes, thinly roll out the white ready-to-roll fondant. Cut out two disks and keep the leftover white fondant. Stick the circles just above the muzzle. Roll out ¼ oz black fondant and cut out two smaller black disks. Stick these onto the white. Flatten two tiny balls of white fondant. Stick these onto the black as highlights. Finish the face by rolling ¼ oz black fondant into an oval for his nose. Stick this onto the muzzle. Paint a mouth using black food coloring.

9 To make the legs, roll two 3½ oz lumps of golden-brown ready-to-roll fondant into chunky carrot shapes. Bend the end of each leg up slightly into an "L" shape to make a foot and stick the legs into place . Cut two round disks out of the remaining black fondant and stretch them into ovals. Stick one on the pad of each foot.

10 For the paws, roll two 2 oz lumps of golden-brown ready-to-roll fondant into two flattish carrot shapes. Rest the hand sections on the bear's tummy (fig 3). Using the back of a knife, press a few lines into each paw.

11 For the final finishing touch, tie a ribbon around his neck.

# Sunbather

*The perfect cake for any beach babe or sun-worshipper – or if mom's greatest wish is a vacation away from it all, then sending a model of her away on a cake could be the next best thing!*

### ■ INGREDIENTS

- 8-in round sponge cake (see pages 94-97)
- 1 quantity butter cream (see page 98)
- Confectioner's sugar for rolling out
- 1 lb 2 oz white ready-to-roll fondant
- Blue food coloring
- 5¼ oz pink ready-to-roll fondant
- 1 oz dark blue ready-to-roll fondant
- 1¼ oz flesh-colored ready-to-roll fondant
- ¼ oz yellow ready-to-roll fondant
- 1 oz brown ready-to-roll fondant
- 1 oz green ready-to-roll fondant
- 1 tbsp white classic fondant icing (optional)
- 2 oz light golden brown sugar

### ■ UTENSILS

- 10-in round cake board
- Carving knife
- Small sharp knife
- Rolling pin
- Water and paintbrush
- Piping bag
- No. 3 nozzle

1 Level the top of the cake if necessary. Turn the cake upside down; slice and fill the center with butter cream. Place on the center of the cake board and spread a thin layer of butter cream on the top and sides.

2 Dust the work surface with confectioner's sugar and knead 1 lb 2 oz white ready-to-roll fondant until pliable. Partially knead in a little blue food coloring for a marbled effect. Roll out, then cover the cake. Smooth the top and sides and trim any excess from the base.

3 For the air-bed, roll out the pink fondant and cut out a rectangle 2¾ in x 6 in. Using the back of a knife, press one line horizontally to mark the headrest, then five lines vertically down the length of the bed (*fig 1*). Lightly moisten the top of the cake with a little water and place the bed in position.

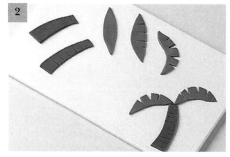

4 For the figure, take 1 oz dark blue ready-to-roll fondant and mold this into a conical shape. Pinch the middle to make a waist (*fig 1*) and stick on top of the air-bed.

5 For the head, roll a ball from ¼ oz flesh-colored fondant. Take another ¼ oz flesh-colored fondant and roll this into a sausage for her arms. Divide this into two and flatten one end of each sausage slightly for the hands. Using ½ oz flesh-colored fondant for the legs, roll into a sausage, divide into two and flatten and shape the ends into feet. Stick the arms, legs and head into position.

6 Roll a small ball of brown ready-to-roll fondant out flat and cut out a thin strip for the hair. Press lines along the length of the strip with the back of a knife. For the sun hat, thinly roll out ¼ oz yellow fondant and cut out a 2 in circle. Stick this over the face. Re-knead the leftover yellow and cut out a slightly thicker circle about 1 in in diameter. Stick this on top of the brim. Decorate with a few balls of pink fondant.

7 For the palm trees, thinly roll out the brown fondant and cut out about 14 small, curved tree trunks (*fig 2*). Press a few horizontal lines into each with the back of a knife and stick these to the sides of the cake. For the leaves, roll out the green fondant and cut out about 28 basic leaf shapes. Make a few tiny cuts in each leaf. Bend each leaf slightly so that the cuts separate and stick a couple to each trunk.

8 For the waves, place 1 tbsp classic fondant icing into a piping bag fitted with a number 3 nozzle. Pipe a few lines around the air-bed. Using a damp paintbrush, pull the icing back from the air-bed (*fig 3*). Butter cream can be used as a softer, but yellower

alternative. Stroke into place with a dry brush.

9 Finally, moisten the exposed cake board and spoon brown sugar around the base.

### TIP

*If you don't want to make up a full quantity of classic fondant icing just for the waves, buy a tube of ready-made icing from the supermarket. This comes with its own set of nozzles.*

# Party animal

*Here's a party animal who's almost completely partied out! If you're sure that they won't take offence, change the hair color to match that of the recipient and substitute his/her favorite tipple for the beer can.*

## INGREDIENTS

- 1 pudding bowl cake (see page 94)
- 1 quantity butter cream (see page 98)
- Confectioner's sugar for rolling out
- 11 oz white ready-to-roll fondant (see page 98)
- 10½ oz pale blue ready-to-roll fondant
- 3 oz black ready-to-roll fondant
- 10½ oz flesh-colored ready-to-roll fondant
- ⅛ oz dark blue ready-to-roll fondant
- ¼ oz yellow ready-to-roll fondant
- 1¾ oz green ready-to-roll fondant
- ¼ oz gray ready-to-roll fondant

## UTENSILS

- Carving knife and small sharp knife
- 12-in round cake board
- Rolling pin and wooden spoon
- Water and paintbrush
- Piping nozzle

1  Check that the cake will sit flat on the cake board when it is turned upside down. If the cake rose slightly unevenly in the oven, you may need to slice a little away from the top. Place the cake towards the back of the board, rounded side uppermost, and slice and fill the center with butter cream. Reassemble the cake and spread a layer of butter cream over the outside.

2  Dust the work surface with confectioner's sugar. Knead 3½ oz white ready-to-roll fondant until it becomes pliable. Roll it out, then place it so that it covers just over half of the cake. Smooth and trim the base.

3  Roll out 3½ oz of the pale blue fondant. Lift and position this so that it overlaps the white. Smooth it into position, and again trim and neaten the base.

4  For the legs, roll 7 oz blue fondant into a thick sausage about 8 in long. Cut it in half. Moisten the board and place the legs into position.

5  Using 7 oz white fondant, make the arms in the same way as the legs. Stick them in position, pointing them forwards towards the front of the board.

6  For the feet, divide a 2 oz ball of black fondant in two and roll each half into a chunky oval shape. Stick one to the end of each foot with water, positioning them in a pigeon-toed fashion (*fig 1*). To add detail, press the back of a knife into the sole of each foot a few times.

7  For the hands, take 1¾ oz flesh-colored fondant and roll into a thick oval shape. Cut the oval in half and using the back of a knife, press four lines into the rounded ends to make fingers. Stick the hands in place. His right one should be flat on the board and his left one on its side and curved, to hold the beer can!

8  To make his face, roll 7 oz flesh-colored fondant into a ball. Flatten the ball into a rounded disk about 41 in in diameter. Moisten the side of the cake and the board in front of the cake with water and lay the disk into position.

9  Make his smile by drawing a line with the back of a knife. For his eyes, roll out ¼ oz white fondant and cut out two small circles 1 in in diameter. Stick these on the face. Roll out ⅛ oz black fondant and cut out two smaller disks. Stick the black circles onto the white (*fig 2*). Complete by sticking on a flattened ball of white fondant as a highlight.

10  For the eyelids, roll out ¼ oz flesh-colored fondant and cut a circle about 1¾ in in diameter. Cut the circle in two and stick one half over each eye to create a droopy-eyed expression.

11  Take a ¾ oz ball of flesh-colored ready-to-roll fondant and slightly flatten it. Stick it in the middle of the face to make his nose.

12  For his hair, roll ¾ oz black fondant into a long thin strip. Press the back of a knife along the length of the strip, then moisten the top of the head with water and lay the strip in place.

13  For the ears, roll ¾ oz flesh-colored fondant into a ball. Flatten it and push the end of a wooden spoon into the center to leave a hollow. Cut the circle in half and stick both ears onto the head.

14  For the hat, roll the dark blue fondant into a triangle. Stick this at an angle on top of his head. Roll the yellow fondant into thin strings and stick to the hat.

15  To make the can, roll the green fondant into a sausage. Flatten both ends. Cut out two flat disks from gray fondant the same size as the beer can. Sandwich the green between the two gray disks and stick a small triangle of black fondant onto the top of the can. Place in position.

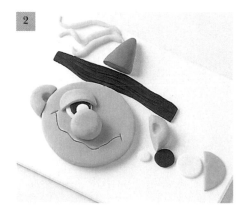

# Deep-sea fishing

Here's one to hook a hungry fisherman! If you prefer a softer sea, substitute butter cream for the classic fondant icing, but use unsalted butter, as this produces a whiter butter cream which takes the color better. Personalize the fisherman if you wish.

## INGREDIENTS

- 1 pudding bowl cake (see page 94)
- 1 quantity butter cream (see page 98)
- Confectioner's sugar for rolling out
- 14 oz gray ready-to-roll fondant (see page 98)
- 6 oz white ready-to-roll fondant
- 2 oz black ready-to-roll fondant
- ¼ oz green ready-to-roll fondant
- ¼ oz flesh-colored ready-to-roll fondant
- Black and blue food colorings
- ¼ oz yellow ready-to-roll fondant
- ½ quantity classic fondant icing (see page 99)

## UTENSILS

- Carving knife
- 10-in square cake board
- Rolling pin
- Cake smoothers (optional)
- Small sharp knife
- Circle cutters or similar for cutting out eyes
- Water, and fine and medium paintbrushes
- Drinking straw
- White cotton thread
- Toothpick
- Small bowl and cake spatula
- Piping bag and no. 3 nozzle, if making waves

1 Turn the cake upside down and carefully carve the front of the cake into a rounded shape. Slice the cake and fill the center with butter cream. Place the cake in position on the cake board and spread a thin layer of butter cream around the top and sides.

2 Dust the work surface with a little confectioner's sugar and roll out 12 oz gray ready-to-roll fondant. Lift this over the cake and ease it into place, using cake smoothers if you possess them to achieve an extra smooth finish on the fondant. Alternatively, use the palms of your hands.

Trim and neaten the base, keeping the excess gray fondant for making the tail. Using the back of your knife, press a curved line into the front of the whale to make a sneaky, smiley mouth (fig 1).

3 To make the eyes, roll out about ⅛ oz white ready-to-roll fondant. Using a circle cutter or a lid of some sort, cut out two flat disks about 1 in wide. (If you cannot find a cutter of the right size, simply squash two small balls of white fondant instead.) Stick one either side of the face with a little water.

Roll out a small lump of black ready-to-roll fondant and cut out two smaller disks (a piping nozzle makes an ideal cutter for these). Stick the black disks onto the white. Flatten two tiny balls of white fondant and stick these onto the black disks to look like highlights.

Finally, to finish the eyes, roll out ¼ oz gray fondant and cut out a disk approximately 1¾ in wide. Cut this in half and stick one half over each eye (fig 2).

4 Make the rocks by partially kneading together 5 oz white fondant and 1¾ oz black fondant (refer to the Wild Animals cake on page 16 for more details if you're unsure how to do this).

Pull off lumps of various sizes and mold these into rock shapes. Make sure that the largest, which the fisherman will sit on, has a flattish top so that he doesn't fall off! Place the rocks to one side.

5 To avoid any accidents, make the fisherman on his rock away from the board. Roll ⅛ oz black fondant into a sausage. Cut it in half for his legs and bend the end of each leg up to make a foot (fig 3). Stick both the feet onto the largest rock. Roll ⅛ oz green fondant into an oval for his body. Stick this above the legs.

> **TIP**
>
> *Remember to remove the thread and toothpick when cutting the cake, especially if there are children around.*

1

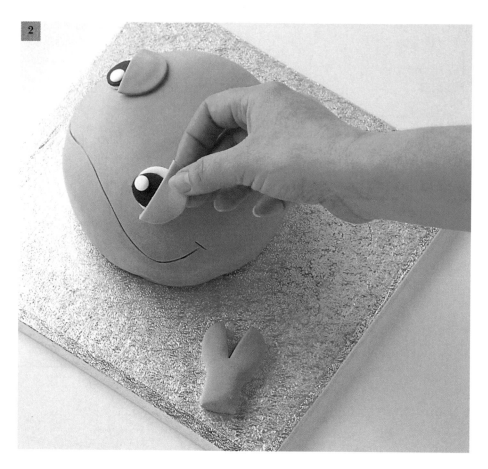

Roll a tiny bit of green fondant into a
sausage and cut this in half for his arms.
Stick one either side of the body so that
they almost meet on his tummy.

6 Make a tiny flesh-colored ball for his head
and stick on top of the body. Holding a
drinking straw at a slight angle, press this
into the lower part of his face to leave
behind a smiling impression. Paint two tiny
dots for his eyes and two little lines for his
eyebrows using black food coloring and a
fine paintbrush.

Stick a tiny ball of flesh-colored fondant
onto his face for his nose and two either
side of the head for his ears. Gently push
the end of a paintbrush into each ear to
add some definition.

Finally, place a final ball of flesh-
colored fondant between the arms for
his hands.

7 To make his hat, roll about ⅛ oz yellow
fondant into a ball. Pinch around the
base, to fan out the fondant into a brim.
Flatten the top and stick it onto his head.
Tie a short length of thread onto a
toothpick and insert this through his
hands into the rock.

8 Make a whale of a tail by rolling about
1 oz gray fondant into an oval shape. Pinch

a "waist" into the middle of the oval and
flatten one of the ends. You should now
have a shape that looks a bit like a violin.
Make a cut down the center of the flat end
and splay the two halves. Cut a small slice
off the other end if necessary to make sure
it can stand up.

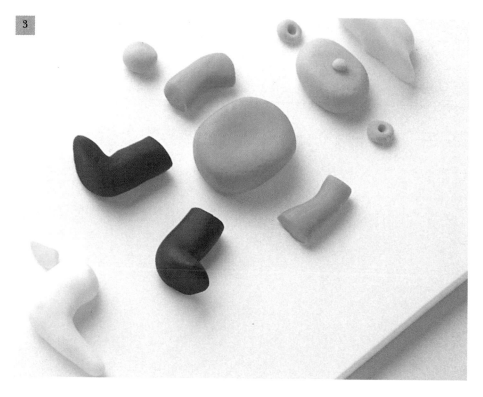

9 Place the classic fondant icing or butter
cream into a small bowl and partially mix in
a little blue food coloring. Spread this
around the cake board with a spatula,
roughing it up as you go.

Place the rocks, fisherman and tail in the
"sea." Add some waves if desired (see the
Sunbather cake on page 82 for details on
how to do this). If using butter cream for
the sea, gently "stroke" the waves into
shape with a dry paintbrush rather than a
damp one.

10 Finally, to make the seagulls, simply roll a
small lump of white fondant into a tapering
sausage shape, then bend this into a "Z"
shape. Add a tiny triangle of yellow for a
beak and two dots of black food coloring
for eyes. Stick one on a rock and one in the
sea. If you've got the time, inclination and
the fondant, you could make a whole flock
and stick some onto the whale's back too.

**TIP**

*For quicker results, use store-
brought fish around the whale.*

# Cookery book

By changing the pictures featured on the open pages of this book to ones of the recipient's favorite hobby, this cake could easily be adapted to suit anyone and any pastime.

### ■ INGREDIENTS

- Confectioner's sugar for rolling out.
- ½ oz black ready-to-roll fondant
- 1 lb 14 oz white ready-to-roll fondant
- 1¾ oz gray ready-to-roll fondant
- 8-in square sponge cake (see pages 94-97)
- 1 quantity butter cream (see page 98)
- Assorted food color pastes e.g. red, blue, yellow, green, brown, black etc
- 2¾ oz blue ready-to-roll fondant
- ½ oz red ready-to-roll fondant
- 1¼ oz light brown ready-to-roll fondant
- Assorted candies, cherries, mini-cakes, etc, for decoration

### ■ UTENSILS

- 12-in round cake board
- Water and assorted paintbrushes
- Rolling pin
- Small sharp knife
- Carving knife
- Ruler
- Palette or saucer
- Clean damp cloth
- Templates for book spine arches if necessary (see page 109)
- Strainer

1 Lightly moisten the cake board with a little water and place temporarily to one side. Dust the work surface with confectioner's sugar and partially knead ¼ oz black ready-to-roll fondant and 1¾ oz gray ready-to-roll fondant into 7 oz of white fondant. Stop kneading before the point at which it all turns a solid gray color (if it does, simply re-knead some more white and black fondant into it).

Roll out the fondant and a marbled effect should develop. Lift and place the fondant on top of the cake board. Continue to roll until the board is completely covered. Neaten the edges and place the board to one side.

2 Cut the cake to shape on a separate cutting board or work surface, slicing about 1 in off one edge of the cake. Place this cut-off strip against one of the shorter sides of the rectangle to increase the width of the book (fig 1). Carefully cut a shallow triangle out of the center of the book as shown to form the spine and discard (or eat!) this piece.

3 Cover the sides and top of the cake with butter cream. Knead and roll out 1 lb 2 oz white fondant and use this to cover the cake. Smooth over the top and sides, starting from the center of the book to expel any air trapped in the spine. To represent the pages, press horizontal lines around the sides using the back of a knife.

4 Knead and thinly roll out 5 oz white ready-to-roll fondant. Measure the top of the cake and cut out two thin sheets of fondant to make the top two pages of the book. Lay and stick these in place and turn the top right corner of the right hand page back slightly (fig 2).

5 Paint your design on top of the cake. To do this, use the food colors like watercolors. You may want to plan out your design on a piece of paper first. Put a dab of color onto a palette or saucer and dilute it slightly with a little water.

If you are right-handed, start by painting the design on the left page first. This stops your hand smudging the painted areas as you work across the book. If you are left-handed, you may find it easier to start from the right. Paint the solid areas of color first (fig 3). Then paint in the outlines using

**1**

## TIP

*If you feel happier wielding a pastry bag than a paintbrush, you could pipe a message onto the cake instead of painting on it.*

black food coloring and a fine brush afterwards. If you try to do the outlines first, you may find that the black bleeds into the colors.

If you make a mistake, simply wash over the error using a clean paintbrush and fresh water and wipe it away with a clean, damp cloth.

6 To "write," simply paint black squiggles across the page, leaving a few indentations to look like paragraphs. Also vary the length of the lines to give the page a more authentic feel. Of course if you're feeling very ambitious you could actually write a message instead.

7 Paint a wash of light brown food coloring around the sides of the book to pick out the pages. Do this by mixing some water into a little brown food coloring and applying it with a large paintbrush or pastry brush.

8 To make the spine of the book, thinly roll out about ¾ oz blue fondant. Cut out two

small arched shapes using the templates, if necessary. Stick one on either side of the book on top of the wash you have just applied. The flat edge of the arch should just rest on the cake board. Roll out about ¼ oz black ready-to-roll fondant and cut out two smaller arches. Stick one neatly on the top of each blue arch.

Paint a line of water around the edge of the book on the cake board itself. Roll 2 oz blue fondant into a thin string and lay this around the cake to look like the book cover.

9 To make the book mark, thinly roll out about ¾ oz red fondant. Cut a strip about 10 in x ¾ in. Cut a small triangle out of one end of the strip. Paint a line of water down the center of the book and lay the book mark carefully in position.

10 Decorate the board using anything you want, such as glacé cherries, small candies, mini-muffins, chewy fruits, raisins and mini-paper cake cases.

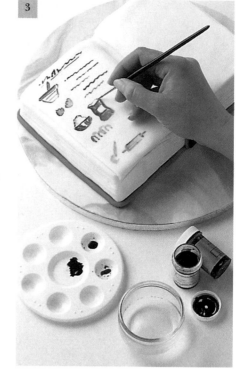

To make a wooden spoon, roll ¾ oz of light brown ready-to-roll fondant into an oval then press a hollow into the center. Make a handle by rolling another ½ oz brown fondant into a sausage about 4¾ in long and press two small dents into the end of the handle using the back of your knife.

11 Finally, to give the whole design an authentic "messy cook" look, place a little confectioner's sugar into a strainer and sprinkle carefully over the cake.

### TIP

*If you don't feel confident about painting, you could cut shapes out of rolled fondant instead or buy the small edible plaques which many supermarkets and sugar craft shops now sell. These can then be stuck on to look like illustrations.*

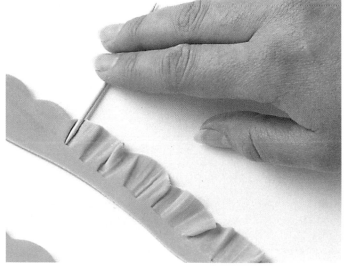

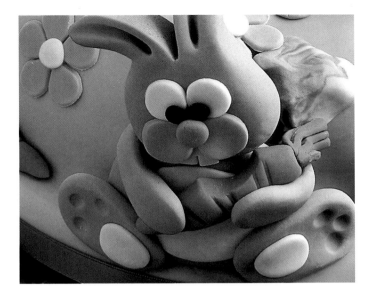

# Techniques and materials

Most of the cakes featured in the previous pages can be assembled from store-bought cakes and, if you're really pressed for time, that's a perfectly satisfactory alternative to baking your own. However, many cake-decorating enthusiasts enjoy baking, and on the following pages I have provided everything you need to know to make a successful cake, whether it be chocolate, sponge, or fruit, and in a variety of shapes and sizes. There are also recipes for different frostings and icings and tips to save you time and money. Finally, I have explained — with clear step-by-step photographs — the basic techniques that will enable you to put together a party cake in no time at all!

# Basic recipes

IF YOU ARE GOING TO SPEND TIME MAKING THE OUTSIDE OF A CAKE LOOK SPECTACULAR, IT IS WORTH MAKING THE SAME EFFORT TO INSURE THAT THE INSIDE TASTES WONDERFUL TOO. THESE RECIPES HAVE BEEN TRIED AND TESTED ON FRIENDS AND FAMILY ON NUMEROUS OCCASIONS AND GET THE THUMBS UP EVERY TIME. BOTH THE MADEIRA AND THE CHOCOLATE CAKE WILL FREEZE WELL (UNDECORATED) FOR UP TO THREE MONTHS.

## Madeira sponge cake

This is one of my favorite recipes as it is so quick and easy to do – you just throw everything in the bowl together and mix. The cake it produces has a firm yet moist texture and is excellent for carving into irregular shapes.

| | | | | |
|---|---|---|---|---|
| **Square pan** | | 6 in* | 7 in | 8 in |
| **Round pan** | 6 in | 7 in | 8 in | 9 in |
| **Self-rising flour** | 1½ cups (6 oz) | 2 cups (8 oz) | 2½ cups (12 oz) | 4 cups (1 lb) |
| **Superfine sugar** | ½ cup (4 oz) | ¾ cup (6 oz) | 1½ cups (10 oz) | 1½ cups (14 oz) |
| **Soft margarine** | ½ cup (4 oz) | ¾ cup (6 oz) | 1¼ cups (10 oz) | 1¾ cups (14 oz) |
| **Eggs (medium)** | 2 | 3 | 5 | 7 |
| **Milk** | 1 tbsp | 2 tbsp | 3 tbsp | 3½ tbsp |
| **Baking time (approx.)** | 1–1¼ hrs | 1¼–1½ hrs | 1½–1¾ hrs | 1¾–2 hrs |

\* **PUDDING BOWL AND LOAF PAN CAKES** – if you are baking a cake in a 1¾ pint pudding bowl or 2 lb loaf pan for cakes such as the Twitcher (page 54) or Sports Car (page 62), follow the recipe amounts for the 6 in **SQUARE** cake and grease and line the bowl/pan as usual.

### Method

1  Grease and line the relevant cake pan or bowl and pre-heat the oven to 300ºF.
2  Sift the flour into a mixing bowl and add all the other ingredients. Bind all the ingredients together carefully, using a slow setting on your mixer, then once the ingredients have combined, increase the speed and beat for one minute.
3  Spoon the mixture into the prepared baking pan and smooth the top.
4  Cook in the center of the oven for the specified time. Test the cake by lightly pressing the center. It should spring back and the top should be golden brown. To be extra sure, insert a skewer. If it comes out clean, the cake is cooked. Leave in the pan for five minutes, then turn out to cool on a wire tray.

### Variations

It's easy to vary the flavor of the cake. Add the zest of a lemon or orange to the mix before cooking for a citrus touch. Alternatively, a teaspoon of almond extract or 2 oz of shredded coconut can add a hint of the Caribbean.

# Chocolate sponge cake

The secret of a good, strong chocolate cake is to use good, strong chocolate in the baking. Use chocolate with a high percentage of cocoa solids (preferably 70 percent). This recipe is superb because the cake it produces has a soft, velvety texture yet is strong enough to withstand being carved into shapes. A crust will form on the top as it cooks. Slice this off and discard, or sell to the highest bidder before decorating.

| Square pan | | 6 in | 7 in | 8 in |
|---|---|---|---|---|
| Round pan | 6 in | 7 in | 8 in | 9 in |
| Butter | 6 tbsp (3 oz) | ½ cup (4 oz) | ¾ cup (6 oz) | 1 cup (8 oz) |
| Superfine sugar | 3½ tbsp (1¾ oz) | 5½ tbsp (2½ oz) | ½ cup (4 oz) | ¾ cup (5 oz) |
| Eggs (medium), separated | 3 | 4 | 6 | 8 |
| Semi-sweet chocolate | 5 oz | 6 oz | 8 oz | 10 oz |
| Self-rising flour | ¾ cup (3 oz) | 1 cup (4 oz) | 1½ cups (6 oz) | 2 cups (8 oz) |
| Confectioner's sugar | ¼ cup (1 oz) | ¼ cup (1 oz) | ⅓ cup (2 oz) | ¾ cup (3 oz) |
| Baking time (approx) | 40–55 mins | 45 mins–1 hr | 1–1¼ hrs | 1–1¼ hrs |

## Method

1 Pre-heat the oven to 350°F. Grease and line the relevant pan and separate the eggs.
2 Melt the chocolate either in a small bowl over a saucepan of boiling water or in a heat-proof bowl in the microwave.
3 Cream the butter and superfine sugar together until light and fluffy.
4 Beat in the egg yolks and, once they are mixed in smoothly, add the melted chocolate.
5 Set the mixer to a slow speed and carefully add the flour.
6 Scrape the chocolate mixture into a spare bowl and quickly wash and dry the mixing bowl. It is important to get rid of any grease. (If you have a spare bowl for your mixer, just swap them over.)
7 Attach the beater to your mixer and beat the egg whites into stiff peaks. Beat in the confectioner's sugar.
8 Re-attach the beater to the mixer and slowly mix the chocolate mixture into the egg whites. Pour the mixture into the baking pan and bake for the required time.
9 Due to the crust, it may be difficult to tell if the cake has baked from touch alone, so insert a skewer or knife. If it comes out clean, the cake should be ready. Turn out and cool on a wire tray.

# Fruitcake

Although it's tempting to buy a fruitcake, especially at Christmas, it means you miss out on two wonderful benefits. First, the sumptuous cooking smells of cinnamon and spices filling the house and, second, the chance to stir the mixture and make a wish!

Don't try to skip double-lining the side and base of the pan with waxed paper or wrapping a double layer of brown paper secured with string around the outside – it really does protect the outside of the cake as it cooks.

| Square pan | 6 in | 7 in | 8 in |
|---|---|---|---|
| Round pan | 7 in | 8 in | 9 in |
| Currants | 1 cup (5 oz) | 1 heaped cup (6 oz) | 1½ cups (7 oz) |
| Golden raisins | 1 cup (5 oz) | 1 heaped cup (6 oz) | 1½ cups (7 oz) |
| Dark raisins | 1 cup (5 oz) | 1 heaped cup (6 oz) | 1½ cups (7 oz) |
| Crystallized peel | ¼ cup (1 oz) | 3 tbsp (1½ oz) | ½ cup (2 oz) |
| Halved glacé cherries | ⅓ cup (2 oz) | ½ cup (2½ oz) | ¾ cup (3 oz) |
| Brandy | 4 tbsp | 6 tbsp | 8 tbsp |
| Butter | ½ cup (5 oz) | 1 heaped cup (6 oz) | 1½ cups (7 oz) |
| Soft dark brown sugar | 1 packed cup (5 oz) | 1 heaped cup (6 oz) | 1½ cups (7 oz) |
| Eggs (medium) | 3 | 4 | 6 |
| All-purpose flour | 1½ cups (6 oz) | 1¾ cups (7 oz) | 2 cups (8 oz) |
| Mixed spice | 2 tsp | 1 tbsp | 1 tbsp |
| Lemons (zest only) | 1 | 1 | 1 |
| Ground almonds | ¼ cup (¾ oz) | ⅓ cup (1 oz) | ½ cup (1½ oz) |
| Flaked almonds | ¼ cup (¾ oz) | ⅓ cup (1 oz) | ½ cup (1½ oz) |
| Cinnamon | 1 tsp | 1 tsp | 1½ tsp |
| Baking time (approx) | 1½–2 hrs | 2–2¼ hrs | 2¼–2½ hrs |

## Method

1 Place all the dried fruits in a mixing bowl. Pour over the brandy. Stir and cover, and leave overnight.

2 Grease the cake pan. Double-line the inside of the pan with waxed paper. Tie two strips of brown paper around the outside of the pan and secure with string. Pre-heat the oven to 300°F.

3 Cream together the butter and sugar, then beat in the eggs. Mix in the sifted flour, spices, and ground almonds.

4 Stir in the soaked fruits, lemon zest, and flaked almonds.

5 Spoon into the pan, level the surface and bake. Check the cake about 15 minutes before the cooking time is up. If the top seems to be browning too much, place some waxed paper over the top. To test the cake when its cooking time is up, insert a skewer. If it comes out clean, the cake is baked. If not, place the cake back in the oven and test again at 15-minute intervals.

6 Allow the cake to cool completely in the pan before turning out and removing the paper.

7 To store the cake, pierce the top of the cake with a toothpick a number of times and drizzle a little brandy into the holes. Double-wrap the cake in waxed paper and then in aluminum foil. Store in a box or tin (never a plastic storage box) and "feed" about once a week with a little brandy. Maximum storage time is about three months.

# Microwave cakes

Although personally I don't think you can beat the real thing, microwave cakes do have their place. Well, with only four minutes' cooking time you can't really go wrong! They do have a slightly different texture to a cake baked in a conventional way, and because they don't brown on top like ordinary cakes, they look a bit anemic when they first come out. But by the time you have smoothed some frosting or icing over them or a thick covering of butter cream, I don't think you'll find anyone complaining. It's also fascinating watching them rise through the window of the microwave – a bit like television! These amounts are for an 7-in round microwave cake pan or a 1¾-pint heat-proof pudding bowl. To make a 8-in round cake, make two cakes using this amount each time and sandwich together. **Never** use a metal cake pan in the microwave oven.

# Vanilla cake

## Ingredients
½ cup (4 oz) butter
½ cup (4 oz) superfine sugar
2 large eggs
1 tsp vanilla extract
1 cup (4 oz) self-rising flour
½ tsp baking powder

1 Grease and line the microwave dish.
2 Cream the butter and sugar together until light and fluffy.
3 Beat in the eggs and vanilla extract.
4 Stir in the flour and baking powder.
5 Spoon into the prepared dish and cook on full power for four minutes. Leave to stand for about ten minutes before turning out.

# Chocolate cake

## Ingredients
½ cup (4 oz) butter
½ cup (4 oz) superfine sugar
2 large eggs
¼ cup (3 oz) self-rising flour and 1 tsp baking powder
¾ cup (1 oz) unsweetened cocoa powder

1 Follow steps 1-3 as for the vanilla cake above (omitting the vanilla extract in step 3).
2 Stir in the flour, cocoa, and baking powder.
3 Cook on full power for four minutes and leave to stand for ten minutes before turning out.

# Stock syrup

This is the baker's secret! If you have to decorate a sponge cake a few days in advance of when it will be eaten, you can use a little stock syrup to ensure that the cake will still be wonderfully moist.

## Ingredients
½ cup (4 oz) superfine sugar
⅔ cup (⅓ pint) water

1 Put the sugar and water in a saucepan and stir together.
2 Heat and bring to the boil.
3 Simmer gently for 2-3 minutes until the sugar has completely dissolved, then allow to cool.

To use, slice the cake in half as normal, but before spreading it with butter cream, "paint" the top side of each layer with the syrup, using a pastry brush. Allow it to soak in slightly but don't saturate the cake. Then spread with butter cream, re-assemble the cake and decorate as usual. For an extra special cake, flavor the syrup with a spirit or liqueur (a dash of rum works especially well with chocolate cake!).

Stock syrup can be stored in the refrigerator in a screw-top jar for up to two weeks. This quantity should be enough for two cakes, but it really depends on the sizes of the cakes, the number of layers you divide them into, and how liberally you apply the syrup.

# Frosting and icing recipes

## Butter cream

As you will notice, I tend to use butter cream a lot on my cakes, the main reason being its versatility. As well as being used to fill and provide a covering for cakes before they are decorated, it can also be colored, stippled or piped. I find it makes the best base for covering a cake because as you spread it, it fills in any little holes in the sponge, leaving a perfectly smooth surface. However, feel free to substitute other fillings, such as jelly, if you prefer.

After you have coated the cake in butter cream, if you have time, place the cake in the refrigerator for an hour so the cake can "set up." This will help to prevent the cake from moving about or collapsing as you cover it, and will also stop the butter cream from oozing out of the sides. When you take the cake out of the refrigerator, spread another thin layer of butter cream over the top and sides of the cake to give the rolled fondant a good surface to adhere to.

Butter cream can be frozen in an airtight plastic container in the freezer for up to three months.

### Ingredients
2 cups (9 oz) unsalted butter (softened)
4½ cups (1 lb 2 oz) confectioner's sugar (sifted)
½ tsp vanilla extract
1 tbsp hot water

1  Place the butter in a bowl and mix until light and fluffy.
2  Carefully mix in the sugar, vanilla and water and beat well. If you beat it on quite a fast speed for about 5 minutes, it should turn virtually white, which is extremely useful if you are going to use it to make waves on cakes such as the Deep-Sea Fishing Cake on page 86.

### Variations
For chocolate butter cream, flavor the frosting with either 3½ oz melted semi-sweet chocolate or 1 tablespoon of cocoa mixed into 2 tablespoons of hot water. For coffee, mix 1 tablespoon of instant coffee into a paste with 1 tablespoon of water and add to the butter cream. Alternatively, instead of the vanilla, substitute a different-flavored extract such as peppermint, lemon, or almond instead.

## Ready-to-roll fondant

Ready-made fondant (also called rolled fondant or sugarpaste) is a great time-saver and can usually be found in the supermarket. It may be called something like "ready-to-roll" fondant. There are a number of brands available and it's worth experimenting to see which one you find easiest to work with. Alternatively, your local cake decoration equipment shop should stock fondant in various colors, or you could try a specialty mail order company.

In case you have problems obtaining prepared fondant, here is a simple homemade version that works just as well as the commercial brands. See page 103 for instructions on coloring fondant.

Homemade fondant using real egg white should be used as soon as possible. If made with dried egg albumen, use within a week.

### Ingredients
4½ cups (1 lb 2 oz) confectioner's sugar
1 egg white (or preferably, the equivalent amount of dried egg white mixed with water)
2 tbsp liquid glucose (available from pharmacies, drugstores, cake-decorating equipment shops and some supermarkets)

1  Place the confectioner's sugar in a bowl and make a well in the center.
2  Tip the egg white and glucose into the well and stir in with a wooden spoon.
3  Finish binding the fondant together with your hands, kneading until all the sugar is incorporated. The fondant should feel silky and smooth.
4  Store immediately in a plastic bag.

## Coloring sugar or shredded coconut

If you are pressed for time, this is a quicker way to cover a cake board than using rolled-out fondant. If colored green, the sugar or coconut makes realistic-looking grass. For a watery look, use blue food coloring.

Place the sugar or coconut into a small bowl and add a small amount of food coloring (use paste, not liquid). Mix in the coloring, adding more if necessary until you achieve the required shade.

# Classic fondant icing

Traditionally, classic fondant icing is made with egg whites. However, because of the slight risk of salmonella poisoning, I try to avoid using real eggs wherever possible. Most supermarkets and all cake-decorating shops sell dried egg white (it may be called dried egg albumen, easy egg or even meringue powder), which produces icing just as good as the real thing. Read the instructions on the package in case the amounts differ slightly from the ones I've given here.

## Ingredients

1 tbsp (½ oz) dried egg white
5 tbsp (2½ fl oz) cold water
4½ cups (1 lb 2 oz) confectioner's sugar

1 Mix the egg white and water together until smooth.
2 Sift the confectioner's sugar into a grease-free bowl.
3 Tip in the egg mixture and if using an electric mixer, beat on a slow speed for five minutes until the icing stands up in peaks.
4 Place the icing in a bowl and lay a piece of plastic wrap directly on top of it. Place an airtight lid on the bowl and keep covered at all times when not in use.

# Gelatin icing

Gelatin icing is an extremely useful icing to have in your repertoire because it sets very hard. It can be used to make things that you want to stick up on the cake (from delicate flowers and leaves to flags, sails, or even turrets as in the Fairy-tale Castle Cake on page 8). It can also be molded over objects and left to take on their shape. It can be colored in the same way as ready-to-roll fondant and also has the added benefit of being usable right away.

TIP: If, when you come to use it, you find that either the gelatin or modeling icing has become too hard, you can soften it by microwaving it on full power for just 4–5 seconds.

## Ingredients

4 tbsp water
1 sachet (approx 1 oz or enough to set 1 pint) gelatin powder
2 tsp liquid glucose
4½ cups (1 lb 2 oz) confectioner's sugar
1–4 tbsp cornstarch

1 Place the water in a small, heat-proof bowl. Sprinkle the gelatin over the top and leave it to soak for about two minutes. Sift the confectioner's sugar into a mixing bowl and make a well in the center.
2 Put about ⅜ in water into a saucepan. Stand the bowl in the water and heat gently until the gelatin dissolves.
3 Remove the bowl from the water and stir in the liquid glucose. Allow to cool for a minute.
4 Tip the gelatin mixture into the center of the confectioner's sugar. Using a knife, begin to stir it in. When it has bound together, knead it into a bread-dough consistency, adding cornstarch as required. Store in small plastic bags until needed.

# Modeling icing

There is a vegetarian equivalent of gelatin available, but even though I have tried three times, I cannot manage to make a modeling paste of usable quality. Therefore, I have included this recipe which uses gum traganth (a powder that comes from a tree). The only slight disadvantage is that at present you can only obtain the gum from specialist cake-decorating shops (find your nearest in the phone directory or see the suppliers list on page 110). Also, in theory, after you have made up the paste you should leave it tightly wrapped in two plastic bags for at least eight hours. This gives the gum time to work and makes the paste more stretchy and pliable. However, as I never seem to have a spare eight hours, I have used it straight away with perfectly acceptable results. Keep it tightly wrapped when not in use as it hardens very quickly.

## Ingredients

4½ cups (1 lb 2 oz) confectioner's sugar
2 tbsp gum tragacanth
2 tsp liquid glucose
4 tbsp cold water
Cornstarch
(You may find it easier to halve the above quantities and make it in two lots. For the turrets on the Fairy-tale Castle Cake on page 8, you will need to make the full amount.)

1 Mix the confectioner's sugar and gum together in a mixing bowl and make a well in the center.
2 Pour in the glucose and water and mix together. Knead to a bread-like consistency on a surface dusted with cornstarch. Place inside two plastic bags and, if you have time, leave for eight hours before use.

# Basic techniques

FROM DEALING WITH AIR BUBBLES TO GETTING RID OF DUSTY CONFECTIONER'S SUGAR MARKS, THIS SECTION SHOULD HELP YOU TO ACHIEVE A REALLY PROFESSIONAL FINISH.

## Covering a cake

When using ready-to-roll fondant to cover a cake, always roll it out on a surface dusted with confectioner's sugar to prevent it from sticking to your work surface. Never use flour or cornstarch. Roll it out approximately 6 in larger than the top of the cake to allow enough fondant to cover the sides as well. It should be ⅛–¼ in thick. You can either lift and place the fondant over the top of the cake – as you would pastry – using a rolling pin, or slide your hands, palms uppermost, underneath the fondant and lift it, keeping your hands flat. Smooth over the top and sides using the palm of your hand and trim away the excess from the base with a sharp knife (fig 1). For a really professional finish, use a pair of cake smoothers. Starting at the top, run them over the surface of the cake to expel any air and iron out any lumps and bumps (fig 2).

If a large, unsightly air bubble develops, prick it with a clean dressmaker's needle or toothpick held at an angle, then carefully press out the air.

## Covering the cake board

### All-in-one

This is the easiest way to cover a cake board with the cake placed on top afterwards. Moisten the entire board with water and begin to roll out a ball of ready-to-roll fondant on your work surface. Lift and place the fondant onto the board and continue to roll it out just over the edge of the board (fig 3). Run a cake smoother over the surface and trim and neaten the edges.

### The bandage method

This is done after the cake itself has been covered. Run a tape measure around the side of the cake and cut a strip of ready-to-roll fondant that length and slightly wider than the exposed cake board. Roll the fondant up like a bandage and moisten the cake board with water. Starting from the back of the cake, slowly unwind the "bandage" over the board (fig 4). Run a cake smoother over the fondant and trim and neaten the edges.

1

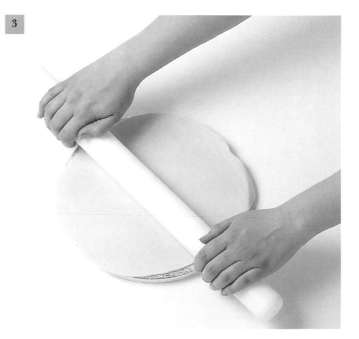

2

3

## The fabric effect

This is also done after the cake itself has been covered. Measure around the cake and cut a strip of rolled fondant about 4 in longer than that length and about 1½ in wider than the exposed board. Moisten the cake board and roll up the fondant like a bandage. Unwind it allowing the fondant to fall into folds around the cake as you go *(fig 5)*. Press down the fondant at the edges and trim away any excess.

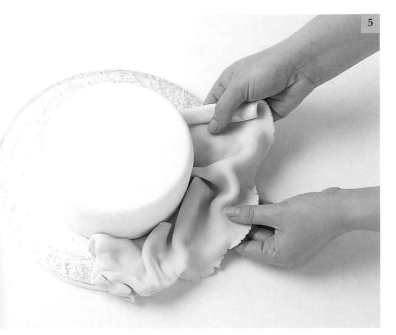

## Covering the board around an awkward-shaped cake

Although covering a board after the cake is in position might look more difficult than covering it all-in-one and placing the cake on top afterwards, it is easier than it looks and has one distinct advantage. Because you slide the rolled fondant up against the edge of the cake, it makes a neater join at the base of the cake.

Moisten the cake board with a little water. Thinly roll out the ready-to-roll fondant and cover the exposed board in sections *(fig 6)*. Run a cake smoother over the surface to flatten any lumps, and trim away the excess from the edges using a sharp knife.

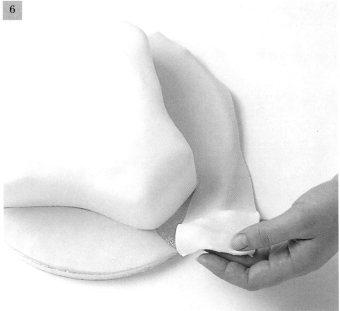

## Edging the cake board

You can neaten the outer edge of the cake board by sticking small strips of double-sided tape around the board and attaching a length of ribbon to it.

# Painting on rolled fondant

Always use food coloring to paint with on cake. The paste colors work best. Also, if possible, leave the covered cake overnight to harden. This will stop you denting the cake if you lean on it.

First brush the area to be painted using a large brush or pastry brush to get rid of any excess confectioner's sugar that could cause the colors to bleed.

Place a few dabs of paste food color on a saucer and "let down" slightly with a little water. If you wish, paint a very light and pale outline of the image on the cake first, to use as a guide. Then fill it in.

Paint on the cake as you would watercolor, mixing the colors to achieve different shades. If painting a heavy black food coloring outline around your images, do this after you have painted the middles. (If you do it first it will bleed into the central color.)

1 Cut some waxed paper into a triangle.

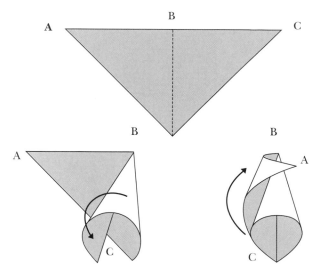

To remove mistakes, gently rub and break up the painted error using a soft paintbrush dipped into clean water. Then wipe away with a clean, damp cloth.

# Making a piping bag

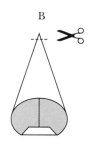

2 Pick up corner "C" and fold over, so that "B" forms a sharp cone in the center.

3 Wrap corner "A" around the cone.

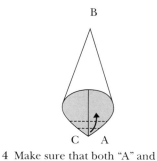

4 Make sure that both "A" and "C" are at the back and that the point of the cone is sharp.

5 Fold points "A" and "C" inside the top edge of the bag to hold it securely. Snip off the end and insert a piping nozzle.

# Hints and tips

● A lot of the hard work can be taken out of kneading almond paste by heating it for a few seconds in a microwave. However, don't overdo it or the oil in the center of the almond paste will get very hot and can give you a nasty burn.

● After you've painstakingly covered your cake with rolled fondant, you might find that an unsightly air bubble has appeared on the surface. Simply prick the bulge with a clean dressmaker's pin or a toothpick and gently press the area flat.

● Get rid of any dusty confectioner's sugar marks after you have finished by wiping away with either a clean, damp cloth or paintbrush. Be careful when cleaning dark colors such as red, black, or dark green as they bleed easily.

● Plastic wrap can not only be used to wrap the rolled fondant but, scrunched up into a ball, it can act as a support for things that are drying.

# Modeling rolled fondant

## Coloring

8

When coloring ready-to-roll fondant, always try to use paste food colors. Liquid coloring tends to make the rolled fondant soggy, especially if you are trying to achieve a deep color. Apply the color with a knife or toothpick and knead in. Most of the colors wash off easily, but to protect your hands and especially nails from staining, you could wear rubber or plastic gloves when coloring the fondant.

It is also possible to color white fondant by mixing it with colored fondant. For instance, knead a small lump of black fondant into a large chunk of white to produce gray.

To achieve a flesh tone for modeling people, the best color I have found for white tones is paprika food color paste. This can be found in all cake-decorating equipment shops, but if you cannot find it, knead a little pink and yellow fondant into some white. For darker skin tones, color the fondant with dark brown food color paste or knead white and brown fondant together. For Asian tones, I use autumn leaf food color paste mixed with a little paprika.

It is best to make up all your colors before you start on a cake and to store them in small plastic food bags when not in use. When you have finished your cake, keep it out of direct sunlight or you may find some of the colors fade before the party.

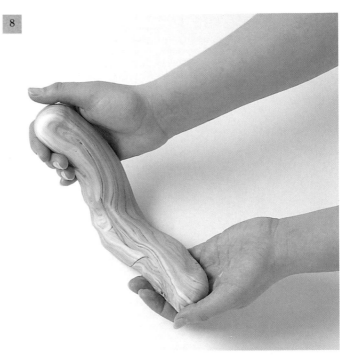

## Woodgrain effect

Woodgrain is an easy effect to achieve and can be done in two ways. One way is to roll a lump of white ready-to-roll fondant into a sausage and apply dashes of brown food coloring with a knife (*fig 7*). Alternatively, roll a couple of lumps of brown and white fondant together into a sausage. Then fold the fondant in half and roll it into a sausage again. Repeat until you see a streaky, wood effect appearing (*fig 8*), then roll it out and use as usual.

## Marbling

Like all the best tricks, this looks stunning but is in fact extremely easy to do. Simply take a ball of white ready-to-roll fondant and partially knead in a small ball of colored fondant or a few streaks of food coloring (*fig 9*).

9

7

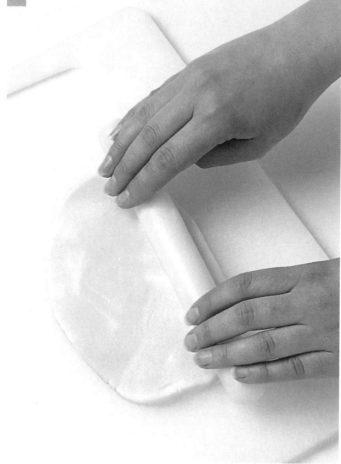

# 10

Then simply roll out the fondant as usual (*fig 10*). If you go too far and the rolled fondant turns into a solid color, simply reverse the process by partially kneading some white fondant back in and rolling out again.

# Cleaning and rectifying mistakes on rolled fondant

To clean any mistake made when painting with food color, gently rub the error with a paintbrush dipped in clean water to dissipate the color. Then wipe away with a clean, damp cloth.

To remove dusty confectioner's sugar marks from the finished cake, simply wipe them away with a soft, damp paintbrush.

# Making figures

Although they may initially look complicated, if you take the figures apart (*figs 11 and 12*) you will see that in fact they are comprised of very simple shapes – usually just a head, body, legs, and arms. Once you have mastered the basic components you can place them in any position you wish, although it is much easier to make a sitting or lying-down figure rather than a standing one. Set them on top of the cake itself surrounded by other "props," such as on the Handyman Cake on page 14 or in an armchair. Another fun way to present figures is to stick them around the sides of the cake. You can then use the sides of the cake for additional support.

Stick the figures together using water. The secret is not to use too much, especially for small items such as ears, otherwise they will just slide off the head.

When it comes to the clothes, you can paint patterns with food coloring or add fine details such as buttons made out of flattened dots of fondant or circles pressed into the fondant with an implement like a drinking straw.

To check whether the proportions of a figure are anywhere near accurate, try to imagine how the character would move with the limbs that you've given him. If he stood up, would his legs be too short? Can he scratch his nose with his hands?

When it comes to the facial details, there are many ways to give your figure expression (*fig 13*). The eyes can be comprised of just the most minimal dots and lines, or they could be painted with food coloring or built up from small disks of colored rolled fondant. Usually, the ears and

top of the nose should be level with the eyes. Think about it – it would be impossible to wear glasses if they weren't!

For maximum cuteness, children and cuddly animal types usually have bigger eyes than adults.

The mouth can be painted or made by pressing something small and circular, such as a drinking straw, into the rolled fondant to make a smile or a frown. Make a small hole with the end of a paintbrush and your figure will look instantly surprised.

To make the changes, I have tried to use different methods of making faces on different cakes. Don't be scared of taking an element from one cake and using it on another.

To achieve a certain expression, it is sometimes easier to draw it out on a piece of paper first. You may also find it helpful to use a mirror to see what your own features do if you pull your face a certain way.

When it comes to the hair, again there are many ways of making this. It could be piped or smeared on in classic fondant icing or butter cream. It could be cut out of strips of rolled fondant. Base the hairstyle on that of the recipient and use the method most suited.

Add any distinguishing features such as glasses, beards or mustaches and as any great cartoonist does, exaggerate (without being too cruel, obviously!).

# Making animals

As with the figures, if you actually take a model of an animal apart, you will see that it comprises extremely simple-to-make shapes. For instance,

the dog (*fig 14*) is made from a couple of conical shapes stuck on top of each other and decorated with two oval ears and a few spots. The cat is even simpler, made from a sausage of ready-to-roll fondant curled up to look as though the cat is sound asleep, with just a pair of ears pinched out of one end.

If you are making a whole cake in the shape of an animal, it is worthwhile making a small model out of rolled fondant first. This allows you to experiment with proportions and colors without wasting vast amounts of materials. Making a small model will also often give you an idea of how the final full-sized cake could be improved.

# Basic equipment

STRAINER  Vital for sifting flour and confectioner's sugar. Also a useful tool for making bushes or hair by simply pushing a lump of rolled fondant through the mesh.

MIXING BOWLS  Even the simplest cake uses more than one bowl, so a good selection of bowls is useful.

CAKE SMOOTHERS  By using a smoother like an iron, and running it over the surface of a covered cake, small bumps and lumps can literally be ironed out. Essential for achieving a smooth, professional finish.

MEASURING SPOONS  A set of standard spoons ensures that you use the same quantities each time you re-make a recipe.

DRINKING STRAWS  These can be used as tiny circle cutters and are ideal for making eyes. Held at an angle and pressed into rolled fondant, they can also be used for making the scales on dragons or snakes.

PIPING NOZZLES OR TUBES  A varied selection is always useful and they can always double up as small circle cutters.  Metal nozzles are more expensive than plastic but are sharper and more accurate.

TOOTHPICKS  They can be used as hidden supports inside models, for adding food color to ready-to-roll fondant, and for making frills and dotty patterns.

TURNTABLE  Although not strictly speaking essential, once you've used one, you'll wonder what you ever did without it.  Cheaper versions are available in plastic.

RULER  Not just for measuring, a ruler can also be useful for pressing lines and patterns into rolling fondant.

SCISSORS  A decent pair of sharp scissors is essential for shaping ribbons, snipping the ends off piping bags, cutting linings for tins, and sometimes rolled fondant.

TAPE MEASURE  Handy for measuring cakes and boards to ensure that you have rolled out enough fondant to go around.

COOLING RACK  Available in all shapes and sizes, and used for cooling cakes.

SMALL DISHES  Useful for holding water when modeling, confectioner's sugar when rolling out fondant. Also ideal when mixing food color into small quantities of classic fondant icing.

BAKING PANS  A good assortment of shapes and sizes is useful.

ROLLING PIN  A long rolling pin like the one shown will not leave handle dents behind in the fondant. Tiny ones are also available and are handy for rolling out small quantities of fondant when modeling. If you don't possess a small rolling pin, a paintbrush handle will often do the job just as well.

CUTTERS  A vast range is available in both plastic and metal.

SOFT PASTRY BRUSH  It is useful to have two – one for dampening or cleaning large areas, the other for brushing away dusty fingerprints or specks of dried rolled fondant.

PAINTBRUSHES  A selection of various sizes is useful. A medium brush is good for sticking things with water when modeling, and a fine brush for adding delicate detail.  Although more expensive, sable brushes are the best.

SCALPEL  Invaluable when sharp, careful cutting is required such as when scribing around a template.

WAXED PAPER  Used for lining pans, making piping bags, storing fruitcakes, and instead of tracing paper.

WOODEN SPOON  As well as for mixing, the handle can be used as a modeling tool for making folds in rolled fondant.

METAL SPATULA  For spreading jelly or butter cream, mixing color into larger quantities of classic fondant icing, and lifting small bits of rolled fondant.

BREAD KNIFE  A long, sharp serrated knife is essential for shaping and slicing cakes.

SMALL SHARP KNIFE  A small kitchen knife with a sharp, straight blade will become one of your most important bits of equipment.

BOARD  Useful when modeling small items.

RULER

MEASURING SPOONS

STRAINER

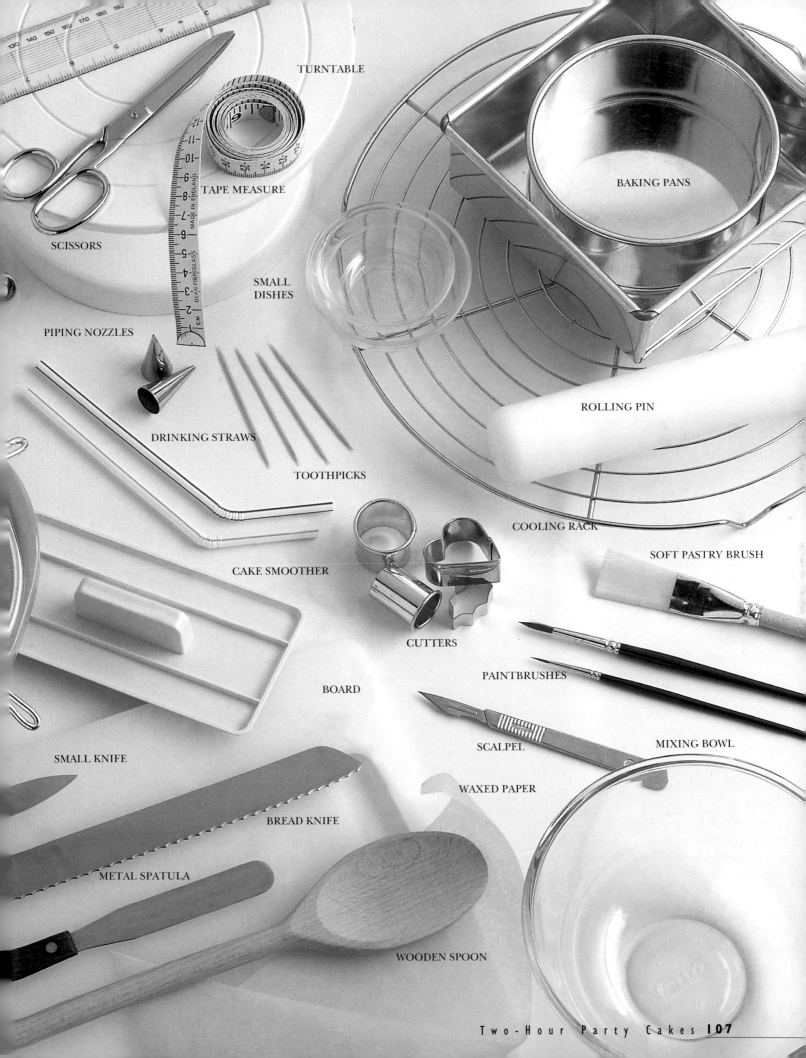

SCISSORS

TURNTABLE

TAPE MEASURE

BAKING PANS

SMALL
DISHES

PIPING NOZZLES

DRINKING STRAWS

ROLLING PIN

TOOTHPICKS

COOLING RACK

SOFT PASTRY BRUSH

CAKE SMOOTHER

CUTTERS

PAINTBRUSHES

BOARD

SCALPEL

MIXING BOWL

SMALL KNIFE

WAXED PAPER

BREAD KNIFE

METAL SPATULA

WOODEN SPOON

# Troubleshooting

## 1 BURNT FRUITCAKE

This can occur if the oven is too hot or if the cake itself is cooked too near the top of the oven. Always try to bake cakes in the center of the oven. If, despite these precautions, the cake appears to be browning too fast, or you prefer a lighter-colored appearance, place a circle of waxed paper with a small hole cut out of the center over the top of the cake and continue baking.

## 2 SPONGE CAKES NOT RISING

Again, the usual culprit behind this is a too hot oven or the cake placed too near the top. It could also be caused by too much egg in the mixture. If you are using large eggs instead of medium, beat the eggs together first, then take out a couple of spoonfuls before adding the rest to the cake mixture.

## 3 FRUITCAKE NOT RISING

The reason for this happening is usually too much flour, so use slightly less in future cakes. It could also be because your ingredients were too cold. Try to use eggs and butter at room temperature.

## 4 READY-TO-ROLL FONDANT/ MODELING PASTE/ ALMOND PASTE TOO HARD

When not in use, always keep these ingredients tightly wrapped in small plastic bags to prevent them from hardening. If a solid crust has formed, there is no alternative but to cut this off and discard. You can microwave any of the above for a few seconds to soften them slightly if you find them hard to knead, but be careful when doing this to fondant as it can cause the fondant to fracture slightly when you lay it over the cake.

## 5 CRACKS AND FRACTURES IN FONDANT

These sometimes occur on the edges of a fondant-covered cake and seem most likely to happen if you overwork the ready-to-roll fondant with too much kneading or microwaving beforehand. Unless you find them particularly offensive, these cracks are usually best left alone or covered with a decoration, but here are two solutions you could try if you wish. On recently applied fondant, take a small lump of the same color fondant and polish it on a shiny surface. Then gently rub the area using small circular motions, and the tiny cracks should disappear. Alternatively, wait until the ready-to-roll fondant has dried, then spread over the cracks a little classic fondant icing in the same color as the heavier fondant. Carefully scrape away the excess using a knife and you should find the fractures have filled.

## 6 WATERMARKS

It is important to remove any accidental splashes of water you may get on your cake as soon as they happen as they will quickly start to dissolve the fondant underneath, leaving an unsightly dent in your fondant. If this does happen in a particularly noticeable area, dab off any remaining water, then gently rub the area with the tip of your finger in a circular motion. Alternatively, use same-color classic fondant icing to fill the hole as described in the previous solution, or place a decoration over the top of the damaged area.

## 7 FRAYED EDGES WHEN CUTTING READY-TO-ROLL FONDANT

To cut ready-to-roll fondant cleanly, you need a small, sharp, non-serrated knife. A scalpel (available from stationery as well as cake decoration shops) is also useful for trimming untidy edges and making intricate cuts.

## 8 AIR BUBBLES

An air bubble trapped underneath a fondant-covered cake has to be removed before the fondant has hardened. Hold either a clean dressmaking pin or a toothpick at an angle and poke it into the bubble. Then gently press out the excess air and run a cake smoother over the surface. If the area still looks unsightly, then do what I do and cover the area with a decoration. This was how I came to have a cat on the armchair cake – and this in fact added extra charm to the cake as well as hiding a problem area underneath.

## 9 COLORS FADING

The usual villain for this is sunlight causing the vegetable dyes to fade. Keep your finished cake in a box, tin (never a plastic container), dark cupboard or somewhere out of strong daylight until it is required.

## 10 FOOD COLORS BLEEDING WHEN PAINTING

This happens when there is excess confectioner's sugar on the fondant surface you are painting. Dust the area first with a large, dry brush (a pastry brush is ideal) before you begin.

## 11 BLOCKED DECORATING NOZZLES

To stop nozzles getting blocked with old icing, use a small paintbrush to give them a good clean when washing up. Also, try to avoid poking things such as toothpicks into the ends as this can force them out of shape. Make sure you sift the confectioner's sugar before making up classic fondant icing to get rid of lumps, and don't mix any crusty bits of dried classic fondant icing into fresh before piping as this can cause blockages too.

## Cake Pans

Cake pans for larger cakes should be made of good quality metal which holds its shape during the baking process, this is especially important when baking rich fruitcakes. Buy the sizes that you are most likely to use regularly, then gradually collect different size pans as needed.

### LINING PANS

For non-stick coated pans, follow the manufacturer's instructions. However, it is advisable to line all cake pans to give cleaner, sharper edges and corners to cakes as well as to prevent the edges of the cake from drying out. Sponge or chocolate cakes will need 1-2 layers of paper, and rich fruitcakes will need 2-3 layers of paper to protect the sides during the prolonged baking times. As extra protection for rich fruitcakes, tie a double thickness of newspaper or brown paper around the outside of the pan or pudding basin — this prevents the sides from forming a hard crust.

# Templates

All templates 100%

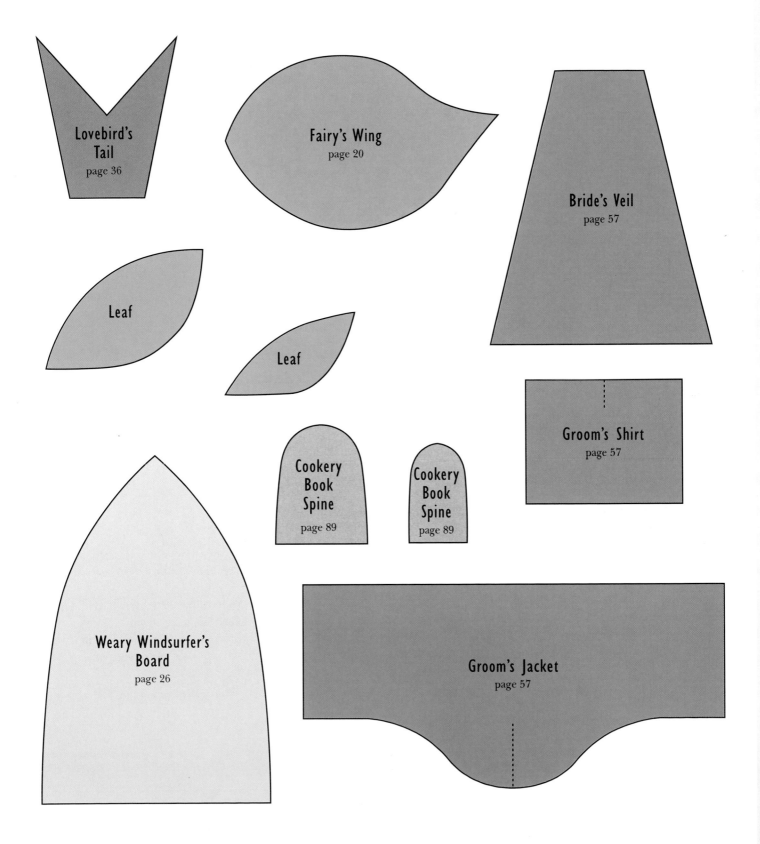

Lovebird's
Tail
page 36

Fairy's Wing
page 20

Bride's Veil
page 57

Leaf

Leaf

Groom's Shirt
page 57

Cookery
Book
Spine
page 89

Cookery
Book
Spine
page 89

Weary Windsurfer's
Board
page 26

Groom's Jacket
page 57

# Specialist retailers

As well as having an extensive range of specialist equipment, some of these shops also offer a mail order service. If none of these are convenient, check your local phone book for your nearest supplier.

Beryl's Cake Decorating & Pastry Supplies
PO Box 1584
N. Springfield
Va 22151
Tel: 1-800-488-2749
Fax: 1-703-750-3779
E-mail: beryls@beryls.com
Webpage: http://www.beryls.com
Catalogue $5.00 refundable with
first order

Bakery Crafts
West Chester
OH 45069
Freephone in the U.S. 1-800-543-1673
E-mail: orders@bkrycft.com

Eileen Walker
Creative Sugar Art
Westworth Drive
Westminster
CA 92683
Tel/Fax: 714-775-7546

Doug Vincent, Trade
Darla'Avra, Retail
D.I.V. Enterprises
Suite 2
6202 South Lewis
Tulsa
OK 74136
Tel: 918-745-0384
E-mail: Cakinbake@aol.com
Websites:
http://members.aol.com/cakinbake/index.htm
http://members.aol.com/orchardste/index.html

Nicholas Lodge
6060 McDonough Drive
Suite D
Norcross
GA 30093
Tel: 770-453-9449
Fax: 770-448-9046
Freephone in the U.S.: 1 800-662-8925

Creative Cutters
561 Edward Avenue
Unit 2 Richmond Hill
ON, L4C 9W6
Canada
Tel: 905-883-5638
Fax: 905-770-3091

American Bakels Inc
8114 Scott Hamilton Drive
Little Rock
AR 72209
Tel: 501-568-2253
Fax: 501-568-3947
Freephone in the U.S.: 800-799-2253